A PLUME BOOK

ASK A QUEER CHICK

Kathleen Schmidt

LINDSAY KING-MILLER received her BA from the University of Arizona and her MFA from Naropa University. She has been writing the advice column Ask A Queer Chick for the Hairpin since 2011, and has contributed to Cosmopolitan.com, *Bitch* magazine, *BuzzFeed*, *The Toast*, and other publications. She lives in Denver with her partner, a lot of books, and two very spoiled cats. She does not have an indoor voice. You can write to her for advice at askaqueerchick@gmail.com. This is her first book.

Ask a Queer Chick

*A Guide to Sex, Love, and Life
for Girls Who Dig Girls*

Lindsay King-Miller

A PLUME BOOK

PLUME
An imprint of Penguin Random House LLC
375 Hudson Street
New York, New York 10014
penguin.com

LIBRARY OF CONGRESS CATALOGING-IN-PUBLICATION DATA

King-Miller, Lindsay.
   Ask a queer chick : a guide to sex, love, and life for girls who dig girls / Lindsay King-Miller.
      pages cm
   Includes bibliographical references.
   ISBN 978-0-14-751678-7 (hardcover)
   1. Lesbians. 2. Dating (Social customs) 3. Interpersonal attraction. 4. Interpersonal relations. 5. Sex. I. Title.
   HQ75.5.K56 2016
   306.76'63—dc23

                        2015018936

Printed in the United States of America
10   9   8   7   6   5   4   3   2   1

Set in ITC Esprit Book

This book is for Charlie King-Miller,
because of everything.

Thank you, tall face.

Contents

Introduction
How Do You Know You're a Queer Chick?

In January of 2011, I began writing the advice column Ask A Queer Chick for the Hairpin, a women's website that had recently launched and had already become something like an intimate party for all the smartest ladies you know— the kind where you drink mojitos with mint someone grew in her garden and get a little too tipsy and end up in a friendly but intense argument over fine points of feminist theory. Back in the day, the Hairpin featured a smorgasbord of advice columns to suit almost any conundrum that might present itself, but none specifically targeted the trials and tribulations of LGBTQ women and the folks who love them. I had never written an advice column before, but as soon as I pitched the idea to then-editor Edith Zimmerman, she was eager to get it going. The column's name and the mascot, a fluffy baby chick with a pink bow on its head, were her idea.

Initially, I had some concerns that it would be difficult to collect enough questions to keep Ask A Queer Chick going on a regular basis, and I even considered writing a few fake letters myself based on Past Lindsay's relationship troubles. But as soon as the first column was published, emails came rolling in. It turned out there were quite a few queer chicks reading, and they had questions—boy, did they. The last few years have been a time of exhilarating highs and disheartening lows for the LGBTQ community. With the legal and social climate surrounding queer issues changing so quickly, it was hard for young people to figure out which way was up, much less navigate the obstacle course of coming out and finding love. Dating, sex, being a person in the world—these are things most of us learn by example, from big sisters and older friends and classmates in school. We need the guidance and wisdom of someone who's already lived through it, but for queer people, those role models are often difficult to find, if not totally nonexistent.

That's what this book is here for. No, it won't tell you foolproof ways to meet hot, available women (although I can tell you that my friend Mickey introduced me to the person I ended up marrying, so maybe hit her up). Instead, it will talk you through some of the major roadblocks you might face on your journey through the joy and heartache of queerness, and offer time-tested tips on confidence, communication, self-advocacy, and generally being the best possible version of yourself, so that when you find the person who makes your heart (and genitals) sing, you can sweep her off her feet. Whether you're struggling with discovering who you are, coming out, hookups, breakups, or anything in between, *Ask a Queer Chick* is here to help you get through it with style, wit, and self-love.

I've been answering your questions for four years, from "Did I wait too long to come out?" to "How should I introduce my girlfriend to my homophobic parents?" to "Is it okay to wear nail polish if I'm gonna, you know . . . ?" I've struggled with all these issues in my own life, and I know the feeling of wishing your heart came with an owner's manual. You've been told over and over that "it gets better," but that doesn't necessarily mean it gets any easier. So you like girls, but does that make you bisexual, lesbian, gay, queer, pansexual, or just curious? What about all those secret code words and gestures that every girl but you seems to know already? And now that marriage might be on the table, all your (cool) relatives are probably lining up to ask when you're going to walk down the aisle, even if you have no idea whether you ever want to get married. What's a lady-lover to do?

In *Ask a Queer Chick*, you'll learn the answers to all these questions and more, from social etiquette (dating your friends' exes, you'll be glad to learn, is *much* more acceptable among queer folk than in the straight community) to sex toy etiquette (rechargeables make you look environmentally conscious and therefore more attractive). We'll talk about how to get dates (an obviously gay haircut isn't required, but let's be honest, it helps) and the basics of relationship maintenance (stand between her and your craziest relative when you bring her home for Christmas).

Ask a Queer Chick will also guide you through some of the less sexy aspects of being queer, like what to do when coming out might mean losing your job, and handling your relationships with bigoted family members. We'll talk about the legal protections at your disposal, what to do when they don't work, and how you can give back to the community. We'll chat about biphobia in both the straight and gay communities, and how to fight it. We'll also discuss the particular challenges queer trans women face, and how cis women can help.

Is This Book for Me?

Throughout *Ask a Queer Chick*, I'll be addressing most of the common—and more than a few of the uncommon— questions I've received in my years dispensing advice. I've abandoned the Q-and-A format for a more general approach, and all of what you'll read here is new writing, though I've touched on many of these topics before. But before we really get into it, there is one topic I want to address right up front. By far the most common question I encounter is some version of the following: "I'm starting to suspect that my sexual orientation and/or gender are not entirely standard, but I'm not sure. Aren't LGBTQ people supposed to know who they are, from diapers on? How do I know whether I'm gay or bi or queer or maybe genderqueer, or if this is just a phase? Who the hell am I?"

First, some bad news: I don't know! I have no psychic powers, nor does this book include a handy Myers–Briggs- style test to determine the truth of your orientation, gender, or identity. Who you are and what you call yourself is something that only you get to, or can, decide.

Now for the good news: You don't have to know yet, either! The words we use to describe ourselves—"straight," "gay," "bi," "trans," "fluid"—are all just approximations; none of them really captures the complexity of our glorious and specific lives. They're ways to describe how you feel and what you do, and most important, they're something you get to choose. There is no right or wrong answer.

Some people will try to convince you that you have only one true identity, and that your job is to find it, possibly by acquiring and following some sort of Lord of the Rings–style treasure map. These people may be either well-intentioned or malicious, but they are definitely not correct. You're not born with a single identity that is perfect and immutable. The core of who you are doesn't change, but how you feel, what you do, and what you call yourself may vary based on your experiences, your stage of life, even your location.

If there's a word that you think might suit you, try it on for a week or a month or a year, and see how it feels. Maybe it will be a perfect fit; maybe it will be a little too tight in the shoulders and you'll want to trade it in, or at least make some alterations. Or maybe it will feel great at first, but you'll start to feel a bit of a pinch as time goes on. All of these things are okay! Exchanging one word for another doesn't necessarily mean you were wrong the first time; it just means that you're growing and changing and trying new things and learning more about yourself. That's something to be proud of.

Having an identity that feels right, that feels true, can be a great source of confidence and strength, and knowing others with the same or similar identities can create a sense of much-needed community, as well as the opportunity to work together to meet common goals and overcome common obstacles. However, the pressure to know what your identity is, to pick a label with absolute certainty and commit to it, never wavering, for the rest of your days, can sometimes be counterproductive. It doesn't matter if you're not sure, right now, whether you're gay or queer or pansexual or straight or homoromantic or any of the fascinating and nuanced words that humans have come up with to describe how they feel and what they like to do, because the feeling and the doing are the only parts that really count.

If you've picked up this book and you don't already identify as a member of the LGBTQ community, you're probably either related to me (hi, Aunt Bobbi! Thanks for being so supportive! Don't read Chapter 4), or your feelings (or doings) have been kicking up some questions in your life. I encourage you to embrace those questions, and follow them where they lead you, without worrying overmuch about what to call yourself in the meantime. Listen to your heart, even when it isn't making much sense; that's how you learn to speak its language. And remember that defining your identity is, in the long run, actually one of the less difficult challenges you'll ever face on your quest to obtain lifelong happiness.

A Note on the *T* Word

It's fairly common to lump the issues faced by transgender people in with those faced by gay, bi, and queer people under the catchall umbrella LGBTQ, or sometimes LGBTQIA (the last two letters standing for "intersex" and "asexual," respectively). This can be useful in terms of creating solidarity, but it can also elide the fact that the challenges of being trans are not always the same as the challenges of being attracted to your own gender.

As a cisgender queer chick, I am not qualified to write in

depth about trans issues, so while some of what I have to say will apply to the whole LGBTQIA community, this is primarily a book for women who date and/or sex up other women. If you're a trans chick whose sexual and romantic compass points dudeward, you may find certain sections helpful, but a lot of the relationship advice isn't going to be relevant to your life. If, however, you're a gay/lesbian/bi/queer trans woman, this book is for you as much as for anyone else. In several places, you'll find sage wisdom from other queer trans women who were kind enough to let me interview them on the particular joys and struggles of being a trans lady who digs other ladies. All girls who like girls are extremely welcome at this party.

With That Said . . .

If you're here, you're at least an honorary member of our happy little club, so enjoy yourself! At the end of the day, it's not about what you call yourself or how many Tegan and Sara lyrics you remember; it's about figuring out what you want and going after it, as bravely and honestly as possible. And then figuring out that, no, that's not actually what you want at all, and starting all over again from square one—and enjoying yourself along the way.

Ask a Queer Chick

Chapter 1

∽

Coming Out

For some people, coming out is the first stage in a life-long journey of queer adventures; others don't get around to it until they've already been partaking of queer relationships and subcultures for years. Most of us within the LGBTQ community have come out and will continue to come out many times, and in many ways, throughout the course of our lives. It can be a daunting process, so this chapter is here to help you handle its highs and lows, whether you're coming out for the first time or the fifteenth.

When Should I Come Out?

The first—and by far the most difficult—step in the coming-out process is deciding whether you need to come out in the first place, and if so, what to come out as. In other words, you have to figure out who you are, what you want, and the words you're comfortable using to describe those things. This may involve reading some books, talking to out LGBTQ people you know, or getting by with a little help from Google—or all of the above. Unfortunately, it's an essentially solitary process, and one that I can offer you little help in getting through. But the nice thing is that once you've done it, the hardest part is over.

Which is not to say that the next part is easy. Once you've made up your mind that you belong somewhere within the kaleidoscope of identities that is the LGBTQ community, there's a complicated calculus that goes into deciding the right time to come out. Every one of us has to figure it out for herself, but here's the simplified version: You should come out when the problems caused by staying in the closet are bigger than the problems that would be caused by coming out.

The downsides of coming out are obvious; in fact, you've probably had a stress dream or five about them: rejection, alienation, having to pretend to like *The L Word*. There are even times when it's downright dangerous to come out, which we'll discuss later in this chapter.

But staying in the closet has its drawbacks, too. Many closeted queers feel a lot of insecurity in their relationships with friends or family members, because they're withholding what is, for most of them, a key part of their identities. They begin to ask themselves questions like "How can I trust someone to love me if they don't really know me? What if someone finds out? What will they say?"

In addition, it's awfully hard to get laid when you're closeted. Because, listen, do you know who queer chicks do not go around hitting on? Straight chicks. We all went through a phase where we had a crush on a straight girl, and it was totally heart-wrenching. It devastated our confidence and our self-respect, and we've sworn on a stack of Sarah Waters novels that we will never go there again. So if you ever want to know the sweet touch of someone else's boobs, coming out is definitely going to be your best bet.

Whenever you start to feel as if you just can't take the secrecy—or the celibacy—anymore, here are some options to consider.

The One-on-One

This is the classic coming-out move. You sit down with someone you care about, pour them a glass of wine (because unless they have a drinking problem, emotional revelations are always better with wine), look into their eyes, and with as little preamble as possible say "I'm gay." Or "I'm bisexual," or "I'm transgender"—whatever truth you've been holding inside. Be prepared to explain your preferred terminology and why you chose it. If you've been keeping secrets about your relationships or other important facets of your life because bringing them up would out you, now is the time to mention them.

Do everything in your power to keep yourself from apologizing. I know it's tempting, especially if the person you're talking to gets upset, but apologizing tells them you've done something wrong, and you haven't. You don't have to be sorry for not coming out sooner, either; it's okay to keep that information to yourself until you feel safe and comfortable disclosing it.

This technique is a winner because it's simple, it's intimate, and it gives you the chance to have a nuanced conversation. The person you're coming out to can ask questions, and you can explain anything you need to. You can also include more than one person in the conversation, of course, but it works best if everyone involved already knows each other well—you probably shouldn't invite your boss or your BFF from college to be present when you come out to your parents.

In some ways, this is the scariest method of coming out, because the possibility of rejection or cruelty is so immediate. It also gives you plenty of opportunity to back out, which can be a positive or a negative, depending on your point of view. And of course, if you plan on coming out to everyone in your life this way, it's probably going to take you a few months— and many gallons of wine.

The Hallmark

Coming out in writing is a popular plan B. If you don't live near the people you want to talk to, putting your disclosure down on paper feels more real and more definite than saying it over the phone. There's also the benefit of not having to be present when they find out, which, if you suspect they might not react well, is a major selling point.

Writing a letter or a card also lets you put as much time and thought as you need into getting the words just right. In person, we all know that no matter how many times you practice your monologue in the mirror, people are going to interrupt and throw you off your stride. With a written disclosure, they can't get a word in edgewise until you've finished saying what you need to say—and if you fumble it on the first try, you can always go back and do it again.

You can even write a cute greeting-card-style poem, if you think your intended recipient would be amenable to it. You can't buy a "Guess What, I'm Gay!" card at your local drugstore (you *can* buy coming-out cards online, but most of them are kind of boring and devoid of personality), but don't let that stop you from crafting your own! You can even borrow this charming poem my BFF wrote in high school for a friend of ours to use when coming out to his sister (feel free to customize as appropriate):

Roses are red
Violets are blue
You like boys
And I do, too!

The biggest downside here is the delay. While your letter or card is winging its way through the mysterious ether of the postal service, you will probably be going out of your mind with anticipation and anxiety. On the upside, you can save time by printing multiple copies of your letter and sending them to everyone in your address book. You could even let this double as your Christmas card and save money on stamps!

The Status Update

Social media is already changing the coming-out game, and our future LGBTQ kids will have options we never dreamed of when it comes to announcing their orientations or identities. (Or maybe not—perhaps by then we'll be living in a utopian society where no one ever has to come out because no one makes assumptions about anyone's sexuality or gender, and thus our kids won't feel pressured into cisgender heterosexuality by default! We can always dream.)

Today, the most useful new coming-out tool is the Facebook status update. When your social media network asks "What's on your mind?" you might as well tell it! "What's on my mind, Facebook, is that I'm just as queer as a three-dollar bill. Anyone know good places to meet cute girls?"

The pro column for this strategy is similar to the one for sending a card or letter: You can take as long as you need to get the wording just perfect, and you don't have to look anyone in the eye at the exact second they find out you're not straight. It has one up on the postal service, though, in that you can see people's responses immediately, thus cutting way down on the waiting-and-freaking-out part of the process.

On the downside, coming out to everyone all at once will make it more difficult to customize what you want to say based on your audience. Also, as everyone knows, the semi-anonymity of social media tends to bring out a certain evanescent douchebaggery in some individuals, so be vigilant about your privacy settings and make sure that no one you don't want to share your news with can see it. Another downside is that if some of your loved ones are less open-minded than others, there's the disheartening possibility of a debate starting in the comment thread where you've just shared the deepest truth of your soul, so tread carefully.

You can, of course, mix and match these approaches as desired—perhaps a sit-down with a few of your closest friends, a thoughtful letter to your parents, and then a social media announcement for more distant family and casual acquaintances. Or you can just reset your "interested in" widget and let that speak for itself. There's no wrong answer here, so feel free to get creative!

Text Message, Gchat, Etc.

Girl. Don't.

My Coming-Out Story, or, What Not to Do

It's the year after I graduated college, and I'm visiting my family for Christmas. My sweetheart, Charlie, is flying in from Tucson in a week's time to spend New Year's Eve with me; we've been together only two months, but it already feels like the most serious relationship of my life. Before Charlie arrives, though, I have to tell my dad and brothers something important. We're in the car on Christmas Eve, on the way to our traditional lunch with our entire Denver-based family—my uncles and aunts and grandmother and cousins—and on impulse, I decide that now is the time.

"I have something to tell you guys," I say, "and I need you to not be dicks about it."

"You know that's not something we can promise," says my brother Kevin, who is seventeen.

I laugh and sigh at the same time, then say, "I told you about Charlie, who's coming to visit me from Tucson. Well, the thing is, Charlie isn't a guy. He's actually, um, more like . . . a girl."

There's a pause while my dad and brothers digest this information. Then Kevin says, "Oh, okay. So you're, like, a lesbian?"

"I don't know," I say. "I've dated guys before. I might date guys again." (I didn't—two and a half years later, Charlie and I got married.) "I think I'm more, like, bisexual, or queer."

"That's cool," says my dad. "You got your grandmother a Christmas card, right?"

Okay, class, here's your discussion question: How many classic rookie coming-out mistakes did I make in this brief anecdote?

First of all, I came out in a moving vehicle. This is a terrible idea. Coming-out conversations are often stressful and emotionally taxing. Sometimes people fight. Sometimes people dredge up old and painful memories just to have more things to throw at each other. And sometimes, when you're in the midst of a fraught interaction like this, you need to bail. It doesn't necessarily mean that your relationship is irreparably damaged; it just means that everyone needs a little bit of time to cool off. But if you're in a moving car, the only way you can get the necessary space is by diving out and rolling onto the side of the road. Lots of us have coming-out scars, but most of us would prefer they not be literal. So, here's the First Commandment of Coming Out: Thou shalt disclose thy orientation in a stationary location with at least one functioning exit.

Second, I came out under a serious time constraint. We were on our way to a family get-together; what if the discussion hadn't gone well? What if my dad and I had gotten into an argument? We would have either had to skip Christmas Eve lunch—a long-cherished holiday tradition—or walk into the restaurant bickering while fifty of our relatives gawked at us in horror. Thus, the Second Commandment of Coming Out: Do it when you know you won't be interrupted for a while. Leave yourself time to talk through all the potential questions and concerns without having to break to order lunch or walk the dog.

Third, and perhaps less obviously, I made my coming out about my partner's identity, not mine. I didn't say, "I am queer"; I said, "The person I'm dating is a girl." This is less a logistical error than a political one and, to some extent, an etiquette one as well. Your coming-out conversation should be about you and the people you're talking to. Don't come out on your partner's behalf unless they've specifically asked you to do so.

When you focus your disclosure on your sweetie's gender instead of your orientation, you give closed-minded friends and relatives the opportunity to see the person you're dating as the "problem." *If only she would break up with so-and-so, everything would be back to normal,* they may think; they may even attempt to sabotage your relationship in the hopes of getting the "bad influence" out of your life. If, however, you make it clear that your queerness is part of your identity and that they cannot reject it without rejecting you . . . well, they might not be any nicer about it, but at least they'll be dealing with the issue more or less head-on.

This ties in with another key point, which is that it's never cool to use your partner as a distraction so your family goes easier on you—even if your partner is not present. Coming out by bringing your girlfriend home, with no prior warning, is also not acceptable. Sexual partners are not singing queer-o-grams, and if there's any chance that your coming-out conversation will turn into a fight, it's your responsibility to protect your ladylove from the cross fire.

Honor the Third Commandment of Coming Out: Always use "I" statements. This isn't about anyone but you. It's one of the few times in life when that's the case, so enjoy it while it lasts!

So What Do I Say?

Everything about coming out is personal and specific, and you should, first and always, do what seems best for you. If you want to come out via skywriting, or by reciting a crown of lesbian-themed sonnets composed for the occasion, those are totally valid moves (and you should send me those poems, because they sound great).

But if you're totally stuck when it comes to approaching the issue, try this easy four-step process: First, tell them what you call yourself. Next, tell them what that means. Then, tell them what's going to change. Finally, tell them how you expect them to behave.

In action, this formula might take the following shape: "Mom and Dad, I'm gay. I'm only romantically interested in women. I'm probably going to bring home a girlfriend in the future, and I expect you to treat her the same way you would if I brought home a boyfriend. I'm happy to answer any questions you have, but I don't want you to feel sorry for me or treat me like I have a disease, because I'm not sad or sick or interested in changing who I am."

Another variation would look like this: "I want you to be the first person to know that I'm a transgender woman. I know that you think of me as a man, but inside I feel that I'm a woman. I'm going to start dressing in a way that matches my gender identity, and sometime in the future I might take hormones or get surgery. From now on, I'd like you to use female pronouns and the name I've chosen for myself when you talk to me or about me."

Obviously, in a perfect world, this would be all the information your loved ones would need, and they would respond with, "Okay. What do you want on your half of the pizza?" Sadly, we do not live in a perfect world, as evident from the fact that Freddie Mercury died before he ever got a chance to record a duet with Beyoncé, and so it is very likely that your audience will have some follow-up questions. Be ready to answer them, or if you're not willing to answer questions, be ready to enforce that boundary—by getting up and leaving, if you have to.

The Worst-Case Scenario

I want to stress that most of the time, when you come out, nothing bad is going to happen. People might be a little awkward, or struggle with your pronouns for a few weeks, but basically everyone will be cool and do their best. Mainstream acceptance of LGBTQ people has made staggering increases in my lifetime—hell, since I started writing this chapter (as I'm typing this, Laverne Cox is just becoming the first transgender woman to appear on the cover of *Time* magazine)—and more and more people are realizing that queer folks are every bit as fun, smart, interesting, and great to have around as anyone else. It is getting easier and easier to come out without significant damage to your health, lifestyle, or relationships. In all probability, the anticipation before you come out will be massively more stressful than the actual event.

However, I cannot tell you with absolute certainty that everyone you come out to will react positively and show you their best selves. I wish I could—I want that for you—but it's just not possible. You might, in the process of coming out, face your own personal worst-case scenario: someone you love rejecting you because of a fundamental aspect of your identity.

If this happens, it will hurt like a bitch, and no amount of reassurance that they're the one in the wrong will take that sting away. But I'm going to say it anyway: If someone is cruel to you or cuts you out of their life because you came out to them, they are the one with the problem, not you.

Pretty much all the advice I can give you boils down to two things, and most of this book will be variations on these two things, with minor adjustments to suit a variety of situations. The first: Take responsibility for your own shit. And the second: Realize that the only shit you can take responsibility for is your own.

It is not your job to convince people to accept you. Nothing about you is unacceptable. You do not need to educate, persuade, bribe, or cajole anyone into believing that you are fundamentally okay. The only thing you need to do is believe it yourself.

If people are cruel or disrespectful to you, do not apologize for who you are; don't grant them the moral high ground even for a moment. Instead, be clear about your own self-respect, and let people know that you won't tolerate being insulted or abused. Enforce your boundaries ruthlessly, and don't let anyone tell you that a moat full of crocodiles is overkill.

You may have to cut ties with people who are important to you if they won't respect your life, your relationships, or your identity. This is really difficult and painful, but it's better than maintaining contact with people who mistreat you. By staying in touch, you send the message that their bad behavior is tolerable. If you remove yourself from the situation, and make it clear that they will not be part of your life until they can stop belittling you, there's always a chance that it will induce a come-to-Jesus moment and they'll work on repairing your relationship. And if not—well, "out of your life" is preferable to "in your life and hurting you."

If you have friends or relatives in common with someone from whom you need to distance yourself, they may try to pressure you into a reconciliation. As much as you can, shut down this topic of conversation before it starts—a simple "I appreciate your concern, but I'm not interested in discussing that" should do the trick. If it doesn't, try again, but leave out the first part. After that, you may have to fall back on the crocodiles.

Finally, if you think coming out may put you in physical danger (violence, being kicked out of your home, etc.), do everything you can to have an exit strategy in place before disclosing. This should include a place to stay, a way of getting there, and a plan for how you'll support yourself, at least for the short term. If anyone makes you feel threatened, call 911 and/or activate your exit strategy immediately—don't wait around to see if things get worse. For more information on the official and unofficial resources available to you, please see Chapter 8.

Third Time's the Charm

While every coming-out story is challenging in its own unique and awful way, there is one particular scenario that deserves a bit of extra attention here: coming out as bisexual. Sadly, lots of people, even people who are nominally "cool with the gays," tend to have a problem accepting bisexuality as the real and valid orientation it is.

Bisexuality isn't always visible the way homosexuality is; if you're queer but dating someone of the opposite gender, people can sort of squint around the edges of your queerness so that it's easier to ignore. This is how I ended up coming out to my mother three times. When I was twelve, I told her, "I think I might be bisexual, and I don't know what to do." She told me it was probably just a phase, and didn't mention it for five years. During that time, I dated boys, kissed girls, and only told her about the boys. When I was seventeen, I told her, "I'm pretty sure I'm bisexual." She told me I probably just thought that because I had so many gay friends, and didn't mention it again for four years. During that time, I dated boys, slept with girls, and only told her about the boys. (Yes, I'm aware that I was part of the problem here.) When I was twenty-one, she asked me if I was dating anyone, and I said, "Yes, and her name is Sarah." That was the one that stuck.

If you come out as bisexual and then date someone of the opposite gender, someone is probably going to sigh with relief and think, *Thank goodness* that *was just a phase,* because a surprising number of people don't understand what "bisexual" means. No matter how insistently you repeat "I am bisexual. I am attracted to people of all genders. Even when I date a person who has only one gender, I will continue to be attracted to people of all genders, because I am totally, one hundred percent bisexual," the second you do anything that could potentially be read as straight, someone will declare you cured. The opposite is also true: If you date someone of the same gender, some people will assume that you're gay, and that being bisexual was just a stage of your coming out. This is called bi invisibility. I wish I could tell you there's a way around it, but frankly, your best bet is to be prepared to gently but firmly correct people for the rest of your life or until the heat death of the universe, whichever comes first.

But I Don't Know What I Am Yet

Here's an approximation of something I see in my mailbox all the time: "Dear A Queer Chick, I think I might be gay or bisexual or some other thing that involves liking girls, but how can I know for sure? I need to be certain in order to come out, but I need to sleep with a girl in order to be certain, but how do I get a girl to sleep with me if I'm not out? What if I never figure out what I am? *Why is life so hard?*" If this is you, here are some things to keep in mind.

First of all, words are an imperfect representation of reality on their best day. Finding a word that accurately symbolizes how you feel and what you want and who you do can be wonderful and validating, but you don't need a word to give you permission. You can still feel and want and do, even if you're not sure what to call it yet. It's okay to dip a toe into the dating pool and make sure the water's as comfortable as you imagine before you plunge all the way in. (Into the water! The metaphorical water. Not someone's . . . you know what I mean.)

If you feel like you need to do some experimenting before you take a big step like coming out, that's fine—you don't have to file a Declaration of Queeritude with everyone you know before you start looking for dates. While trying to stay closeted at home/school/work, you'll probably want to avoid hitting on girls in places you normally frequent. Instead, try a gay bar (or queer youth center, if you're not of drinking age) or an online dating site. If you make a move on someone, there's a good chance that she'll ask how you identify, but never underestimate the power of a shrug and an "I just don't like labels, you know?" to make you seem intriguingly mysterious and nonconformist. (Note: This will only work if you and the person you're courting are under twenty-two years of age; older than that and it will sound pretentious.) Go on a few dates; have a few make-out sessions on dance floors or in the front seats of cars; figure out whether it's as much fun in real life as it is in your head.

On the other hand, you don't have to have any sexual or romantic experience at all before you come out. Your orientation isn't just your history; it's your wishes and desires as well. You can be queer if you've never kissed a girl; you can be bisexual if you've dated only one gender; you can be asexual if you've had sex. If your gut is telling you what kind of person you want to be with, it's probably right, even if you've never been with that kind of person yet. So don't get too attached to the idea that you need to "prove" your identity before you can announce it to the world.

Sure, there will be people who will want—even demand—proof; who will ask you how you can be sure you're queer if you've never had a girlfriend, or how you can know that you don't like boys if you've never kissed one. I wish I could tell you that would never, ever happen to you, but unfortunately, I can't. I can tell you, however, and not for the last time, that *those people are the problem,* not you. Your identity is what you say it is, no matter what experience you have or don't have.

Finally, a lot of people who aren't out yet see coming out as a major transition, after which nothing will ever be the same; that's why they're hesitant to take that step with anything less than absolute certainty. But the truth is, after the big announcement, you'll come out lots more times in your life, pretty much every time you meet someone new. And even among people you already know, it's not like you'll mention it once and then it will never come up again. You'll have many chances to restate, expand on, and define your orientation over time; you're not stuck forever with whatever word you choose today.

Coming Out and Breaking Up

It's heartbreaking but true that sometimes coming out means ending an existing relationship. When you realize that the compass of your heart (or your libido) is pointing you away from the person you're dating, the only thing you can do is end it as soon and as compassionately as possible.

Even if you're not ready to come out, it's never okay to continue a relationship with someone you don't care about the way they care about you. People are very good at sensing when you've detached from them emotionally, and the never-ending dance of *"What's wrong?" "Nothing." "Is something on your mind?" "No, don't worry about it"* will eventually wreck their trust not only in you but in their own perception and instincts. Don't be that person. If you can't say "We're breaking up because I'm gay," you can use one of the ever-popular Generic Breakup Excuses like "I just don't know what I want right now" or "I love you, but I'm not *in* love with you." Your soon-to-be-ex will probably resent the deliberate vagueness, but let's be honest—they weren't going to be thrilled with you anyway.

If you do disclose your orientation to your lover emeritus in the process of breaking up, it might make things easier or harder. They may feel they've been deceived, especially if they've sensed for a while that something was wrong, and if you led them on or lied to them because you weren't ready to be out yet, you owe them an apology. On the other hand, sometimes it's better to hear "I'm breaking up with you because I've realized I can't be happy in a relationship unless it's with a woman" than "I'm breaking up with you because your new haircut is terrible and your jokes aren't funny." Again, don't spend too much time worrying about the best way to break someone's heart. No matter what approach you choose, it's going to suck, so just do the best you can to balance kindness with honesty, and accept that there's no way to prevent feelings from being hurt.

Once the deed is done, it is your responsibility to take it easy on your ex. No matter how well things go or how much you promise to remain friends, being dumped is ego-bruising, and they will need time to recover. That means not using them as your emotional support system while you begin to navigate the exciting world of queerness, and *absolutely* no coming to them with your romantic problems until a reasonable mourning period has passed. No matter how much you care about them and want to remain close, there is no smooth transition from romantic partners to BFFs. The more wounded party needs time to heal, so take your dating woes elsewhere for at least six months, or until *they* start dating someone new.

There's also the unfortunate possibility that even if you want to continue a relationship, your coming out will result in your partner breaking up with you. Even if you disagree with their reasons, everyone gets to decide for themselves what is or isn't a dealbreaker, whether it be gender, orientation, or favorite Spice Girl. Try not to hold it against them (unless they're deliberately hurtful about it, which is never okay). Be glad that you're now free to find someone new who doesn't see any part of your identity as a drawback, but is ready to embrace every incredible and unique facet of who you are.

The Perks of Staying In

Sometimes, coming out is just not an option. If you're working in one of the twenty-nine states where you can get fired for being gay, or the thirty-two states where you can get fired for being trans, your livelihood might depend on your willingness to stay in. If being openly queer would get you harassed at school, persecuted by law enforcement, or kicked out of your house, hiding your orientation or gender isn't lying—it's a survival skill. Passing for straight and cisgender is the right choice if it protects you physically and/or financially. Bear in mind, however, that if you choose to come out—or if you're outed against your will—and suffer negative consequences, neither your disclosure nor your queerness are responsible for any abuse you receive. You deserve to be treated well. Don't blame yourself if other people fail to live up to what you deserve.

That said, if you are in a situation where it's unsafe to come out, you should be actively *planning*—not just wishing—for the day when you can leave. Set money aside for a place of your own. Apply for positions with more open-minded employers. Work hard in school so you'll have lots of opportunities to improve your circumstances. Accepting your current surroundings while you work to create a better life for yourself is great, but giving up and deciding that you'll just have to pretend to be straight forever is not.

When you're stuck and can't see a way out, every problem is crushing and demoralizing. It's easy to feel like the problem is *you*, like there's something fundamentally wrong with the person you are. There isn't—you're a wonderful human being in shitty circumstances, and you *will* find a solution, as long as you keep setting goals and working toward them. It's okay if it's slow, it's okay if it's hard, it's okay if you have unexpected setbacks. Just keep reminding yourself that you deserve a life where your identity is affirmed, validated, and celebrated. And don't let anyone, including you, talk you out of making that happen.

Your Coming-Out Party

Sometimes I imagine what coming out would be like in a perfect world. On your eleventh birthday, Harry Potter style, an owl would appear outside your house (where did it come from? How did it know? These things are and will forever remain ineffable) bearing a certificate suitable for framing: "Congratulations, you're queer!" Your family would be so proud of you—"We always knew you could do it," they'd say—and would present you with cards and gifts and, in some cases, just straight-up cash.

Obviously, it's not that simple, but coming out is a milestone, and I wish we lived in a culture that treated it like one and celebrated accordingly. Sure, coming out is often fraught with pain, self-doubt, and struggle, but that's true of lots of other things people throw parties and give gifts for, like graduating from college, turning thirty, having a baby, or getting married. We are a species that likes to mark life transitions with greeting cards and cake. Why should coming to terms with your gender identity or sexual orientation be any different?

Since there is no long-standing tradition of coming-out parties in Western culture, you're not beholden to anyone— not your grandmother, not Emily Post—to do this any particular way. Take the opportunity to *literally shape the future of queer culture* by throwing the shindig of your idiosyncratic dreams, so that parents of queer kids can pressure them to do the exact same thing a hundred years from now because "that's just the way you're supposed to do it!"

Invite three people over to play charades, or throw an enormous house party with a keg and an all-Beyoncé playlist. Go bowling, or hire a string quartet. Invent a drinking game based on all the things you love about your marvelous, unique self. Create a signature cocktail to mark the occasion. It's your party—do whatever sounds like fun. And welcome to the beginning of your incredible queer life!

Chapter 2

∾

Of Mullets and Motorcycles: Your Guide to the Subculture

This chapter is your passport to Queer Country, a place that looks almost exactly like the world you're familiar with, except that the haircuts are less symmetrical, the emotions are right on the surface, and some of the girls want to date you. Getting your bearings here and making friends with some of its citizens will make your journey not only easier but way more fun. LGBTQ subculture isn't just a tangent to your queer life; if you want it to, it can be an incredible source of inspiration, support, and joy. Have fun exploring!

What Is Queer Culture?

If you're new to this whole shebang (yes, that was a lesbian pun), you may be wondering what it means to be queer, beyond the obvious dating, romancing, and sexing parts. I get a lot of letters from fresh-off-the-press lady-lovers asking, "Do I have to get a fauxhawk now? What about a motorcycle?

Is playing softball mandatory? And how do I find other gay people?"

It turns out that there's a lot more to being a queer chick than just making out with good-looking girls. Through centuries of institutional and personal repression, LGBTQ people have had to create a thriving, joyful culture for ourselves outside of the mainstream—music, writing, fashion, you name it. The more homophobia has tried to squeeze us out, shut us down, and silence us, the more we've responded by carving out our own spaces and making them amazing.

These days, as more and more straight folks catch on to the fact that not only are queer people awesome but we've created a lot of awesome things, the line between mainstream culture and LGBTQ counterculture is becoming ever more blurred. This means, sadly, that the girl with the short hair, Sleater-Kinney T-shirt, and Doc Martens is not necessarily gay; you're just going to have to ask her out and see for yourself. It also means that queer culture is more accessible—and safer to access—than ever. Even before you work up the nerve to come out officially or ask a girl for her number, you can begin to acquaint yourself with queer spaces and people, and start to shape your own identity as a member of the community.

There are two important things to keep in mind as you explore the spaces (both physical and psychological) that we as LGBTQ folks have created for ourselves. The first is that queer culture is optional. The second is that it's powerful.

The only requirement for belonging to the LGBTQ community is that you own your nonnormative orientation or gender history or gender presentation and live in it as wholeheartedly and authentically as you can. You don't have to get a "gay" haircut or buy a Ducati or listen to Melissa Etheridge. If anything that you think of as a signifier of queer culture doesn't sound like fun to you, you're always welcome to skip it and do something you'll enjoy more. Anyone who thinks (or says) that you're less queer because of it is wrong, and also a jerk.

However, identifying with other people who share aspects of your experience, and using that shared experience to create communities and action and art and social change, is incredibly important. Whether it's a weekend-long queer-only music festival or a moment of wordless solidarity with a stranger on the sidewalk, an opportunity for bonding and support can encourage, energize, and sustain you. Don't close yourself off to these connections just because you're afraid of becoming "stereotypical."

Stereotypes and Visibility

When you picture a lesbian, what do you imagine? A girl with a buzz cut, unshaved legs, and an Indigo Girls T-shirt, pulling up to a softball game on her Harley-Davidson? A femme in a vintage shirtdress with sky-high heels and smoky eye makeup? A woman with bright blue streaks in her hair wearing skinny jeans and Chuck Taylors, marching in a rally to raise awareness for homeless trans youth? Does the image in your mind look like someone you aspire to be, someone you aspire to see naked, or someone you never want to be mistaken for?

There are countless stereotypes about queer women,

many of them focusing on excessive masculinity (the "butch dyke"), excessive emotionality (the "processing lesbian"), or excessive resistance (the "radical queer"). In one way or another, the prevailing cultural image of what a queer woman looks, sounds, and acts like tends to be defined by transgression. Lesbian, bisexual, and queer women are expected to break some or all of the unwritten rules that govern femininity in our society.

These stereotypes can be dangerous. Being perceived as a transgressor can get you taunted, harassed, ostracized, and otherwise discriminated against—and the more stereotypically or "obviously" queer you are, the more intense this marginalization can become. Not all of this backlash will come from straight people, either. Within the queer community, some folks will give you shit for being too stereotypical ("You're making the rest of us look bad!"), and others will mock you for not being "obvious" enough ("You're basically a straight chick"). In one way or another, we are all constantly being measured against someone else's standards, and, as often happens when real people are compared to arbitrary, inflexible standards, we are usually found wanting.

It can be tempting, then, to say "fuck your standards" and do everything you can to defy people's expectations of what a queer woman can or should look like. Which is totally cool! Break all the rules, challenge everything, and create new visions for yourself and those around you. Remember, though, that stereotypes make you visible, and visibility matters.

If no one had any preconceived notions of what a lesbian looked like, how would you know that the cool waitress at your favorite indie coffee shop is gay, and how would you enjoy the subtle nod of mutual recognition you two share every morning as she hands you your soy mocha with an extra shot? Being visible as a queer person helps you connect with other members of the LGBTQ community (if you've never received especially good service from a clearly gay waiter, you need to move to a queerer neighborhood). It lets you serve as an ambassador of sorts, proving that queer people are great just by being yourself and doing the things you normally do. And it's an act of resistance: You fight oppression and homophobia by not allowing your queerness to be overlooked or downplayed. All of these things rely on other people's ability to read you as an LGBTQ person.

Your relationship to stereotypes about queerness is ultimately up to you, and you should never give in to pressure to act or dress a certain way just because that's what dykes are "supposed" to do (and you should certainly never, ever date or sleep with anyone who tries to control how you present yourself as a queer person). But I hear from a lot of young lesbians who are eager to prove that they're "not a stereotype," as though wearing boxer briefs and motorcycle boots is the most shameful thing a lady-lover could ever do. At least some of those girls will eventually regret the years they spent avoiding things they actually love because they were afraid of being too obvious. Follow your own path, but make sure that you're doing so because it makes you happy, not because you look down on the equally valid choices of others.

Butch, Femme, and Everything in Between

"Butch" and "femme" are important words in the girl-on-girl community, words with long, rich, and intertwining but distinct histories. Queer women have organized their communities and their politics around those words for much longer than you or I have been alive, and if I were to delve into them with the depth and nuance they deserve, we would be here all day. Let's just agree on these basic definitions of the words as they're generally used nowadays: "Butch" refers to a queer woman with a masculine-of-center gender presentation, and "femme" refers to a queer woman with a feminine-of-center gender presentation.

Since those categories are incredibly broad, lots of folks have taken to adding modifiers in order to pinpoint a more exactly calibrated position on the three-dimensional topographical map of gender ("gender spectrum" is so limiting). There's "high femme," "soft butch," "hard femme," "stone butch," and probably dozens more; if you can't find the phrase that fits, invent one! Or don't. It's perfectly okay to feel that your gender presentation doesn't need a label, just as it's fine to fluctuate between butch and femme depending on the day.

While not every woman in the LGBTQ community vibes with one of those words, they can be useful in defining how you approach gender, visibility, and even relationships. Like most words, they function largely as shorthand: They give you the outline, but it's up to you to fill in the details of the picture.

If you think of gender presentation as a spectrum that

slides from femme to butch, you can picture the queer visibility spectrum lined up almost perfectly parallel, with "femme" and "invisible" overlapping on one end, and "butch" and "visible" on the other. Because the cultural default is to assume that everyone is straight, any woman who doesn't obviously deviate from the norm in dress or do is generally perceived as heterosexual. I have a haircut strongly associated with the queer community—long on one side, shaved on the other—but new people still tend to read me as straight because (most of) my hair is long, and I wear skirts and high heels regularly.

If you're on the feminine-presenting side of the spectrum, you will probably experience what's often referred to as "femme invisibility," also known as the widespread assumption that women who like to wear and do girly things are straight. This can be frustrating for any number of reasons, not the least of which is the necessity of coming out over and over to everyone you meet in your life. Femme invisibility can also make it difficult to get dates—if you've hit on a straight girl once, you never want to risk doing it again—which means queer girls who rock a maxi dress and winged eyeliner generally have to get used to making the first move, or at least dropping lots of hints indicating that they are open to a move being made.

Butch women are much more likely to be read as queer, especially by people in the LGBTQ community and those who have some familiarity with queer aesthetics. Though this means that there's less pressure to come out repeatedly, it can also lead to an increased risk of taking shit from ignorant people who feel compelled to inform you that you look like a lesbian, as though it might have happened by accident. And ultimately, there's nothing you can do to ensure that people will read you as queer 100 percent of the time. My partner has a fauxhawk, rides a motorcycle, wears bow ties and men's vests, and has two tattoos based on Indigo Girls lyrics, and *still* occasionally gets mistaken for straight. So don't spend too much time adjusting your look based on the reaction you hope to get from passersby; just wear what makes you feel confident and comfortable. Reassure yourself that, in the words of the sometimes problematic but occasionally very wise RuPaul, "what other people think about me is none of my business."

Femmes Are from Mars, Butches Are from Venus

Although it's far from mandatory, lots of chicks do gravitate toward butch-femme pairings, with or without traditional gender roles attached. Some butches want to make the first move, be the sexual aggressor, and come home to a femme-cooked meal every night; some femmes want to pursue a high-powered career while their stay-at-home butch raises the babies. Whatever relationship model works best for you is fine, but don't assume that you'll be flawlessly compatible with someone just because she's a femme who dates butches and you're a butch who dates femmes.

In fact, I'll go further than that: Don't assume that you know *anything* about someone based on her gender presentation, except for her gender presentation. The fact that someone identifies as butch or femme doesn't tell you anything about her politics, her favorite band, or how she likes to have sex. Pursuing someone just because she dresses and wears her hair in a way that you find appealing, in the absence of any other knowledge about her character, is dehumanizing and unlikely to get you laid. Sadly, I know more than a few femme queers who fall all over themselves whenever a good-looking butch enters the room—and several very hot butches who could not possibly be more Over It. Take the time to get to know someone as a person before you try to get into her boxer briefs.

On the flip side, if you spend any time at gay bars or other queer-populated spaces, you can't help but notice that sometimes the way a butch interacts with a femme has an undercurrent of what I can only call misogyny. "Butch chivalry" is definitely a thing, and it can be very cute when it comes from a place of respect and equality, but its dark side is an attitude of objectification, possessiveness, and generally looking down on feminine-presenting queer chicks. It's hard to avoid absorbing a little bit of "girl stuff is icky!" from a misogynistic culture, but if you're a butch lady, don't condescend to the femmes in your life or treat them like conquests. Femininity and masculinity are value-neutral, and we're all in this thing together.

Butch-femme relationships can be wonderful; I am in one, and it makes me ridiculously happy every day. But they're not mandatory. If you're a butch who wants to date butches, or a femme who wants to date femmes, or an androgynous person who doesn't care about your partner's gender presentation as long as she can hold her own in a vicious game of Scrabble, by all means pursue that. And if you do find yourself in a butch-femme pairing, remember that your sweetie is so much more than the way she relates to gender, and take care to treat her like a person, not an archetype. Some butches cook gourmet meals (and that's hot). Some femmes ride Harleys (and that's hot, too). All of our differences and idiosyncrasies come together to make the world a more interesting, not to mention sexier, place.

Your Gayest Hair Ever

One of the time-tested, classic ways to mark your allegiance to the queer community is to get a really gay haircut. For many of us, it's a rite of passage. Shortly after coming out, my partner sat down in the salon chair and said, "Make me look like a lesbian." It can be a way of demonstrating disinterest to suitors of the dudely persuasion (although plenty of bisexual and even straight chicks rock alternative-lifestyle haircuts these days) or of advertising your availability to other ladies in the know. It's also simply fun, and freeing, to shake off the heteronormative beauty standard that we're all subjected to and get a haircut that no one is expecting.

I shaved my head for the first time when I was fifteen. I was terrified to do it (my hair was long enough to sit on), but the physical sensation of all that weight leaving my head, and the experience of looking at myself in the mirror and realizing that I looked *tough* and *cool* and that maybe now girls would like me, made for one of the most liberating and thrilling moments of my life. In a society that tells women their hair is the measure of their femininity and their femininity is the measure of their worth, I believe with every fiber of my soul that you—every woman, actually—should get a super-short coif at least once, just to feel how people's perception of you changes. It is strange and scary, and you will feel like a badass for being able to withstand it, which you deserve, because you *are* a badass.

If super-short is not the look for you, there are compromises available, such as the fauxhawk, the mullet (primarily popular among rural queers and women of a Certain Age, but not by any means extinct, as I found out when I attended my first Indigo Girls concert), the pompadour, and the undercut or side mullet, which is my haircut of choice because it allows me to look queer while still having long, flowing mermaid hair. There are versions of these styles available for pretty much every imaginable hair type, texture, color, and length, too. If you see someone who has a coif you covet, don't be afraid to get it just because it might not look exactly the same on you. You'll put your own unique spin on it, and nine times out of ten, it will turn out great. (The tenth time? Well, it'll grow back.)

Having a "gay-looking" haircut can be risky in certain workplaces where a more conservative appearance is expected, or when job hunting. And some people simply don't want to deal with being so visibly queer all the time, or don't feel that the approved dos fit their personal aesthetic. That's totally fine. You don't have to do anything you don't feel comfortable with—and remember, if you're queer, any haircut you rock is a queer haircut.

Gaydar: Separating Fact from Fiction

One of the first questions I ever got when I started writing Ask A Queer Chick was "What's the deal with gaydar, anyway?" This is something many of us wonder about. Is it just intuition? Pheromones? Is it like those whistles that only dogs can hear? Can straight people have it? Can you learn it, or do you have to be born with it?

Well, here's the scoop: Gaydar—the ability to pick gay, bi, lesbian, or queer people out of a crowd—is the learned, not innate, ability to identify traits and mannerisms commonly shared by members of the LGBTQ community. Sometimes gaydar works consciously—"That girl is wearing a Le Tigre T-shirt, has super-short, clean fingernails, and is giving me the serious Sex Eyebrows; I'm pretty sure she's a mo"—and sometimes it's subliminal—"I don't know what it is, but she just seems queer to me."

People who are queer often pick up certain identifying characteristics—like gestures, a certain way of walking or speaking, a style of dress, etc.—that mark them as members of this subculture. Sometimes these mannerisms are performed consciously (which doesn't make them "fake"); sometimes we start doing them without meaning to and cannot shake them no matter how hard we try, as many people who would like to stay closeted a little while longer learn to their chagrin. It can be difficult to articulate what these characteristics are—they're not always flamboyant or obvious—but the more time you spend around queer folk, the better you become at spotting them in the wild.

Once, my partner and I were at a concert with my mom,

and one of the opening acts was a female rapper who set my gaydar whooping. "Think she's queer?" I said.

"Oh my God, so queer," said my partner.

"What makes you think that?" asked my mom. We shrugged. It wasn't anything we could put a finger on—she was just obviously super gay. Two minutes later, the performer said, "This next song is about my ex-girlfriend." I still couldn't tell you how I knew she was gay; sometimes you simply know.

Not every queer person will display the distinctive yet ineffable markings that gaydar picks up on. Conversely, some straight people will. If you don't have a finely calibrated gaydar yet, that's fine, and it doesn't make you any less queer than your pal who can spot bicuriosity from a hundred feet away. You can work on your powers of perception simply by hanging out with other LGBTQ people more often—which, hey, you probably want to do anyway!

Where Do I Find Other Queers?

So you came out, you got your Baby Dyke's First Pixie Cut, and you're ready to start making queer friends and influencing queer people. There's just one problem: You have no idea where to find them.

If you live in a big city, finding other queer folks is as easy as googling "lesbians in Denver." Major metropolitan areas are hotbeds of LGBTQ social life (this is true even if your state tends toward the conservative). Every large or even medium-size city has a gay bar, and while many gay bar scenes are dominated by dudes, they usually have at least one night a month or week set aside for the lady-loving ladies. If your hometown has a dedicated lesbian club, so much the better. It might not become your spiritual home, but it's a good place to start.

If you can't find a gay bar or if you hate the loud-music-and-alcohol culture, there are other, slightly less obvious places to meet queer people. Try any bar or coffee shop with an open mike night; gay women's ears are uniquely formed to deeply appreciate the sound of acoustic guitars, and if there aren't any lesbians onstage, I bet you anything there are a handful in the audience. On a similar note, poetry readings are a weirdly great place to find queer women—I think we're naturally drawn to environments where we'll be rewarded for sharing our feelings. Ask the Internet if there's a poetry slam or open mike near you; it may well become the place you meet (and later process your emotions about) your next three exes.

Feminist and women-owned bookstores are also frequented by queer women of all ages, especially the places that serve tea or locally roasted coffee. As a bonus, while you're sitting around waiting for someone cute to walk in, you can catch up on your Audre Lorde. And be sure to attend their readings or signings; when a gay writer is promoting her latest novel, you'll have a great chance of meeting some smart and sexy literary ladies.

Does your city have an LGBTQ community center? If you don't know, investigate! These venues often have everything from drag shows to free STD testing to group counseling to book clubs. They also usually offer alcohol-free, queer-specific social spaces for the underage, which can otherwise be hard to find.

If you live in a small town or a rural area where the population is tiny, the available queer community is of necessity going to be smaller and probably offer fewer options. Maybe there's a lesbian bar, but they're always showing tennis when you want to watch soccer. Maybe the entire lesbian subculture in your town is three middle-aged dykes with a quilting circle, while you're nineteen and desperately want to find some punk rock chicks to date.

In cases like these, your battle cry must be "Onward to the Internet!" Queer-chick-oriented websites like Autostraddle and AfterEllen and dating sites like PinkCupid can be lifesavers for anyone who has difficulty connecting with people in "real" life (due to shyness, social anxiety, Resting Bitch Face, etc.), especially for folks who are geographically isolated. You can also try Meetup or something similar; maybe there are tons of people near you who would love to get together for margaritas and *Pretty Little Liars* marathons, but none of them know the others exist yet. Take advantage of the technology at your disposal, and if all else fails, start saving up for a move to a big city, where the queers are jumpin' and the rent is high.

Building a Queer Community

Most places with a population over twenty have at least a *little* queer community, but it's not necessarily everyone's scene. "Too much drinking," "terrible dude-to-lady ratio," and "unfriendly to bi and trans folks" are complaints I hear a lot. The good news is, if the perfect queer community for you doesn't exist yet, you can take steps to create it.

Though there are many tried-and-true approaches to finding queers in the wild, don't assume you have to go to an Officially Designated Gay Place to make new friends. If there are cool queer people at your workplace or in your yoga class, ask them where they like to hang out—the answer may surprise you and open up new social possibilities. Or just ask them to come over for board games or movies and bring a couple of friends.

You can also create new venues for queer interaction. I've planned a lot of events in my life, and you'd be shocked how easy it is. Wish there were a girls-only open mike at your favorite coffee shop? Tell the cute barista what you have in mind, and ask her to put you in touch with the owner. Want to start a queer soccer league? Call the parks and recreation department, and ask them how to go about reserving a field. If there's an organization you think should be doing more LGBTQ outreach, hit them up; they'll probably be overjoyed to hear from a community member who wants to get involved! Start a monthly happy hour get-together for the queers at your workplace, and hatch your plans for world domination over vodka sodas and artichoke dip. Tell your favorite salsa club that if they have a Dyke Night, you'll spend every waking moment spreading the word and putting up flyers, and give them the greatest turnout they've ever had on a Monday.

Whatever kind of queer subculture you wish were available, I promise you have the power to make it a reality. Start by finding the community that already exists, and use it as a building block and resource—don't try to pull an entire social circle out of thin air. Be clear about what you want to offer and how it's distinct from what's already out there, and most important, be willing to do the work. If you demonstrate enthusiasm and follow-through (and don't make out with anyone else's girlfriend), queer people will love you and show up to your events, and all of a sudden, you'll be a community leader!

(And please use your newfound power to make sure there are vegetarian food options available at Pride next year. No, funnel cakes do not count.)

Putting the *T* in Community

One of the greatest failings of contemporary queer women's communities has been their lack of solidarity with the gay, lesbian, and bi trans women among us. If your ladies' night or women's music festival has a transphobic, vaginas-only policy (also known as "women-born women," which is both bigoted and baffling), you need to go sit in a corner and take a hard look at your life and your choices.

Let's be super clear: There would be no contemporary LGBTQ rights movement without the contributions of trans women like Marsha P. Johnson and Sylvia Rivera, and any queer community that attempts to exclude trans people is moving in the wrong direction. Trans women, especially trans women of color, face some of the harshest persecution and discrimination of anyone in the LGBTQ community, and given everything they've contributed to the Cause, it's the responsibility of the entire community to stand with them.

Lots of trans women are also sexually and romantically interested in women, and for them especially, queer women's spaces should provide a welcoming and supportive home. It's always shitty to police someone else's gender expression and identity, but it's especially harmful—and, unfortunately, prevalent—to do this to trans people. I chatted about this via email with queer trans writer Gwen Wagner, who says, "As a trans woman, you're held to the most strict standards of gender or 'you aren't a real woman,' but if you gender too hard, then 'you're just a man portraying a parody of womanhood,' so you feel this need to constantly be perfect and pass perfectly." Do your part to fight this unrealistic expectation by never, ever demanding that someone prove her gender to you, through dress, behavior, or anything else. A person's gender is what she says it is, and that's the end of the conversation.

When I asked Dylan Ley, my Twitter friend and an awesome queer trans lady, what queer spaces need to do to make themselves more accessible to trans folks, she said that cis people should "listen to the trans people in that community. Listen to what they have to say, and what their concerns are. Avoid letting cis people speak about trans lives, and especially avoid letting cis people speak over trans people about what matters and what should matter" to trans people. She also points out that it's not the responsibility of trans people to educate their neighbors; if you're a queer trans woman who feels unsafe in your town's LGBTQ social spaces, you can stick around and try to reform them, but it's also okay to walk away and start building a community of your own.

Pride Is Great but Also Sort of Terrible

There are two things every queer person should do at least once in their lives. One is read *Just Above My Head* by James Baldwin, because every human should read that book, because it's spectacular. The other is go to Pride.

You should attend Pride because it's genuinely heartening to surround yourself with LGBTQ people in a positive, supportive environment. You should attend because it's an opportunity to meet people, see cool performances, find out about important issues, and acquaint yourself with some of the resources available to your community. But before you head out, you should be clear about what you're going to encounter there.

Like a lot of queers, I have a complicated relationship with Pride. I don't go every year. I did go this year, primarily for the Dyke March, because my partner and I were bemoaning our lack of queer friends (the struggle is real everywhere) and for some reason thought Pride would be a good place to make some. I've performed at two Pride festivals in two different cities. I sometimes enjoy Pride and sometimes wish I'd stayed home. When I stay home, I sometimes wish I'd gone.

The Pride festivals of today are, in some ways, far removed from their radical roots. This evolution reflects a shift in LGBTQ politics and experiences since the 1970s. Most people who attend these events today are not fighting for their day-to-day survival; they're fighting for greater visibility and equality, which are important but definitely not the same thing. Where Pride was once a site of genuine resistance, it's grown now into something like a caricature of itself, an excuse to be loud and flamboyant and performative—camp rather than genuine subversion.

Don't get me wrong: Camp can be inspiring. Unfettered, loud, in-your-face queerness is beautiful. I love any space that encourages weirdness and self-expression. I saw people at Pride this year wearing everything from rainbow fairy wings to bikinis to superhero flags to elaborate formal wear (at noon on a ninety-five-degree day). I saw tons of queer couples holding hands or engaging in PDA without looking over their shoulders to make sure they were safe. I even saw a gaggle of teenage lesbians having a full-on, graphic processing sesh in the middle of everyone: "I don't hate you, Amanda," one of them said. "I just think that *you* think that I'm not good enough for Stephanie."

This is necessary because even in today's increasingly queer-friendly political climate, most of us still encounter casual homophobia in our day-to-day lives. Plenty of us go days or weeks without ever speaking to another LGBTQ person. Pride is an affirmation that there are a lot of us, that we're here for each other, that our lives and our families and our concerns matter. It's a chance to check in with the community.

But although it's a great opportunity to celebrate your identity with people who understand, it's also usually hot, always crowded, and often overwhelming. The music is loud. The beer is expensive. Actually, everything's expensive—a major driving force behind the increasing mainstream acceptance of queer folks is that big companies have realized we have money, and they want it. So Pride is also plastered in advertising. It's packed with smokers, and most of the food options are basically deep-fried sugar. In other words, it's just like any other summer street fair, except that other LGBTQ people expect you to treat it like a religious pilgrimage to Drunkville with an optional side tour of Regrettable Hook-upsborough.

If you want to get shitfaced and laid at Pride, God knows I'm not going to think less of you for that—it's practically a rite of passage. But with all the madness going on around you, don't get too attached to the idea of forming meaningful long-term relationships. Also, as much as I love the idea of making new queer friends, the truth is that the people you show up to Pride with are probably the ones you'll talk to all weekend. Most folks party with the friends they already have. If you want to use Pride to build your LGBTQ social circle, a better move is to contact the organizers a few weeks or months in advance and sign up to volunteer. Everyone loves a friendly face who's willing to hang up posters and hand out pins.

Don't expect Pride to blow your mind or change your life, but do take advantage of the opportunity to relax and be yourself in a crowd of people who get it.

Keep Your Lesbros Close

When we think about what it means to be queer, it's common to focus on the dating and sexing parts of the equation. After all, that's what makes us queer, right? If it weren't for who we want to see naked, there'd be no difference between us and everyone else.

This is both accurate and incomplete. Having unorthodox

romantic desires is what makes us different, but what we do with that difference is what makes us awesome. That's why we have Pride: We're proud of not allowing ourselves to be beaten down by discrimination, or shamed into silence. We're proud to have turned our marginalized status into a thriving and powerful sense of community. You should be proud of that, too, and you should avail yourself of the opportunities it offers.

Having queer friends is important. Your straight friends rock, but if you make even one or two killer LGBTQ friends who understand you on a fundamental level, it will transform your life. Lesbros—queer women you love deeply but platonically—are the sturdy foundation upon which your incredible future will be built.

Starting out on this adventure, focus on making friends first, finding dates second. Romantic relationships, especially the ones that happen in adolescence and early adulthood, are tempestuous, chaotic, and prone to ecstatic highs and devastating lows. It's almost impossible to avoid being swept up in them, but you need something stable to come back to when that beautiful girl crushes your heart into powder beneath her vintage heels. You need someone who understands what you're going through when you deal with homophobia from your family or in the workplace, someone you can bond with over why Faith from *Buffy the Vampire Slayer* is your root, someone who will turn you on to queer writers and musicians you've never heard of. You need someone who will pick you up when the world or your own heart knocks you down. When you find a person like that, do whatever you can to keep her by your side.

Sometimes it's easy to see the queer community as a non-stop game of musical girlfriends, a romantic competition in which you can't relax, even if you're winning. Try to resist that perception. Yes, you and your friends will probably find yourselves vying for the affections of the same girl at some point; it happens to almost everyone. But take deep breaths and keep things in perspective. Twenty years from now, you and your BFF will probably be sitting on the porch drinking mojitos and saying "Remember the time we almost got into a fight over that girl with the weird butterfly tattoo? What was her name again?"

You can make it through this crazy world alone, but it's harder and way less fun. Everything is better when someone knows your story and has your back. Start looking for your queer community, because once you find them, everything will get a lot easier.

Chapter 3

∞

Don't Stare at Her Rack Too Much, and Other Advice on Dating

"Yeah, yeah," I can hear you saying, "community and solidarity and all that. But come on, when am I going to get a girlfriend?" This chapter is here to hold your hand through all the tumult and tribulation of finding someone to date, winning her over, and figuring out whether she's really right for you. It's going to be scary but also wonderful, like a roller coaster that might one day help you raise your children. You probably won't find the perfect person right away, but try to enjoy the journey—you'll get to know yourself, have adventures, and collect some great anecdotes you can use to wow the girl of your dreams when you finally find her. Dating isn't always fun, but at least it's rarely boring.

Starting the Conversation

If you've followed the steps in Chapter 2 and started establishing yourself within a queer community—or begun to create the community you want to see—you're going to have plenty of opportunities to meet potential dates. When you spend a lot of time in queer social spaces, chances are good that you regularly cross paths with people you might want to see naked. Even if you don't actively seek out other LGBTQ folks, you probably run into cute girls at school, work, the grocery store, etc., and are wondering how to parlay your shared enthusiasm for organic raisins into a passionate make-out session and/or lifelong commitment.

As a lady looking to date other ladies, you'll want to ascertain early on whether the potential recipient of your attentions is also queer, but you don't want to open with "Hi, I think I've seen you here before. Do you like girls?" Putting sexual orientation front and center gives the impression that you see her as a sex object rather than a human being you're interested in getting to know.

So when you want to chat someone up, think of her as, well, a human being you're interested in getting to know. Introducing yourself to a stranger can be intimidating (which is a nicer way of saying "sweaty, pulse-pounding, and goddamn terrifying"), but it does get slightly easier the more you practice it. Find some kind of common ground to get the ball rolling; this can be as simple as "I hate how long the lines here get in the morning" or "Where did you get those cool earrings?"

If her response indicates that she's open to communicating with you—that is, if she looks at you and speaks in complete sentences—you can keep the conversation going by asking questions or offering information about yourself. If, however, she looks away, gives you a one-word answer, or otherwise indicates an unwillingness to socialize, don't push it! No one owes you her companionship just because you overcame your nervousness to seek it out. And of course, people in public spaces who are wearing earphones, texting, or already speaking to someone else should never be interrupted under any circumstances, unless it's to politely inform someone that her purse is on fire. (I feel that public reading is a "don't talk to me" signal as well, but I know some people feel that a book can be a conversation starter, so *maybe* it's okay to say "I love that book!" and proceed according to her response. But don't do it to me.)

Once you begin to hit it off with a hot girl, you'll want to drop a hint or two that your intentions are sexy in nature, especially if you met in a neutral location where neither of you can reasonably assume that the other is queer. See if you can find a natural way to disclose your orientation ("Oh, that's a cool T-shirt! My ex-girlfriend was really into that band"). Then, go ahead and ask for her number. If she gives it to you, she's either extremely clueless or queer and available. Calling her up a few days later to ask her out for coffee should clarify the issue once and for all.

Femme Invisibility and Your Love Life

Trying to meet women in a world that's designed to help women meet men can already feel like a death slog across muddy ground in too-small stilettos. The added factor of being the Incredible Invisible Femme makes it all the more difficult. Why isn't that hot girl picking up on the psychic signals you're beaming in her direction? You've glanced at her across the coffee shop *twice* in the last half hour! And while you were staring at your laptop, too intimidated to look at her a third time, you nervously tapped your fingers and *your ring finger was pointing right at her.* Doesn't she understand this means you're gay and single and she should come over and introduce herself?

If you are a femme-of-center queer woman with anything less than flawless self-confidence, you probably experience this whirlwind of emotions so regularly you could set your stylishly understated watch by them. Flying under the gaydar means you usually have to be the one to make the first move. This can be daunting, but just like anything involving human interaction, the more you work at it, the easier it becomes.

You can also up your odds of being the flirtee once in a while if you spend a fair amount of time in queer-focused spaces (see Chapter 2). And Internet dating makes for a solid alternative to standing around in your home-silk-screened "I Need a Girlfriend" T-shirt and hoping someone applies for the position. But honestly, the best way to get what you want is to walk over there and offer to buy her a chai.

The Trials and Tribulations of First Dates

Okay, so the thing you desperately hoped for has happened: Either you worked up the courage to talk to the gorgeous girl in the Doc Martens, or (hallelujah!) she put the moves on you, and now you're going on an actual no-kidding date, the way our ancestors did back before hookup culture and sexting and these kids today with their loud music. Congratulations! A few things to keep in mind:

1. Dress and act like yourself. Don't put on a ton of makeup if you normally go au naturel; don't worry about coming up with "interesting" topics of conversation that don't reflect your actual interests. You're not auditioning for the role of Perfect Generic Dating Person. You're getting to know someone and determining whether you'd enjoy spending more time together. If you're intractably nerdy and would rather discuss *The Silmarillion* than the Grammys, there's no point boning up on pop culture you're not interested in to attract a non-nerdy girl with whom you have nothing in common. If you live in jeans and T-shirts, you need someone who likes you in jeans and T-shirts, not someone who only digs chicks in suits. Don't wear something that's dirty or full of holes, but aim to look and act like the best possible version of *you*, not someone you saw in a magazine one time.

2. The person who initiated the date pays. (This is, for some reason, the thing straight people bring up most frequently in opposition to same-gender relationships. *Who would pay for the dates?* You guys, women have been allowed to have jobs and money for at least ten years now. It's really fine.) Here's why: When you ask people on dates, you're requesting the pleasure of their company for an activity of your choosing, but you have no way of knowing whether that activity is within their budget. Maybe your favorite restaurant costs as much as they normally spend on groceries for the week. It's not polite to request an overview of their finances before you suggest hanging out, so invite them on a date that you can afford—even if that's just coffee or going for a walk in the park and feeding the geese.

Since getting the entire world to catch on to this policy is taking some time, if you are the invited party, it's not a bad idea to offer, one time, to split the check. If your date takes you up on it, cool; if not, don't insist. Check-wrestling is no one's favorite contact sport.

If someone invited you out and paid for the date, and you feel uncomfortable with the thought of not paying your own way, you can suggest another activity as your treat. That's what happened on my first date with my now-spouse: I asked Charlie out to dinner at my fave Greek place, and paid; after we ate, since we were still enjoying each other's company, Charlie suggested we go to a carnival—her treat. That was the best first date of my life, by the way, which leads me to:

3. Do something you actually enjoy. Again, you're trying to figure out whether you and this other person make a good match, not trying to impress her with character traits you don't actually possess. You don't have to be worldly or sophisticated or outdoorsy or artistic if those things don't do it for you. If your ideal date is eating cheese that's been set on fire and then riding some roller coasters, go for it, because there's someone else out there who wants the exact same thing and you deserve to find her.

4. Keep it one-on-one. I know the "group date" thing has been around since at least the 1950s, but just because something's existed for a long time doesn't mean it shouldn't be wiped from the face of the earth like the plague it is (see also: racism, animal abuse, mayonnaise). If your friends are present, it's hard to focus on getting to know your date. If *her* friends are present, you're going to feel way more on display, anxious, and judged than you otherwise would. If the idea of spending one-on-one time with somebody doesn't sound like fun, err on the side of not dating her.

The Setup

Even in today's world of OkCupid and Tinder and HER and bisexual speed dating, there's a very good chance that at some point in your romantic career, you will find yourself staring across the table at a moderately priced Thai place into the eyes of your sister's roommate's friend from work, and you will realize that the inevitable has happened: You have been set up. (It can't be an accident that the colloquialism for "arranging a date between two strangers" is the same as the one for "framing someone for a crime they didn't commit.")

Blind dates are cringe-inducing a vast majority of the time, but it's probably worth sticking it out through the appetizers on the off chance that this is one of the exceptions. What you want to figure out is, do you actually have anything in common with this person, beyond being gay?

For some reason, though almost nobody likes being set up on dates, almost everyone likes to set others up. Straight people in particular are constantly announcing that they know someone you'd be perfect with, and offering "Um, well, she's queer" when pressed for an explanation.

But sometimes even these ill-conceived matchmaking attempts work out. In college, a girl from my linguistics class asked if I'd help set her friend up with my roommate. Since she had barely even had a conversation with my roommate, I surmised that this was a case of "They're both gay men—why wouldn't they like each other?" and declined to get involved. She approached my roomie directly, gave him her BFF's number, and they dated for two years. Sometimes magic happens when you aren't expecting it.

More often than not, of course, it doesn't—but then, that's also true when you go on an OkCupid date with someone who shares your political views and taste in music down to the last Bratmobile B-side. Romantic and sexual chemistry are strange and elusive creatures that seldom come when they're called. If you're looking for a sweetheart and not having much luck, what the hell, you could do a lot worse than getting sushi with your aunt's coworker's bisexual daughter. At the end of the day, it's better to have sushi with someone who doesn't turn out to be your true love than not to have sushi at all.

How to Tell If She's into You

So you've been on a couple of dates, and you really like her, and you have a lot of fun together, and maybe you've made out a couple of times or had sex in the ladies' room or whatever, but how do you know if she, like, *likes* you likes you?

I have some bad news for everyone who has sent me this question and also everyone else who has ever tried to form a romantic connection with another human being: There is no foolproof way to know for sure. Everyone processes and expresses their emotions differently, which means that those magazine articles and self-help books professing that you can read your significant other's intentions by how often she blinks or the angle at which she crosses her legs are total, shameless lies. All you can really do is trust your gut and look for patterns. If you feel bad or anxious about your relationship, even if you can't put your finger on exactly why, you should probably bounce (see "The Red Flag of Nuh-Uh" later in this chapter for more details). If you feel happy and are bubbling over with excitement whenever you think about it, you should keep on keepin' on.

That said, there are a few signs to look for early in the relationship that hint it's going to last. Above all else, someone who *really likes you* is nice to you. I know it sounds ridiculously simple, but I've forgotten about this basic requirement more than once, and I'm willing to bet you have, too. If she never asks about your day, laughs at your jokes, gives you compliments, or does something sweet just because, either her heart's not really in it or she's a jerk. Move on.

Someone who *really likes you* wants to spend time with you, even if you're not doing exciting Dating Things like going out for fancy meals or sharing a scenic bike ride. The person who wants to hang out while you get your oil changed and pick up your prescriptions is the one who's in it for the long haul.

Someone who *really likes you* is also apt to go out of her way to make you happy, even if it involves doing something she's not particularly into. Charlie hates horror movies, but I love them. A few weeks into our dating situation but pre–Going Steady, I mentioned that the local art house was having an all-night slasher flick scream-a-thon. Charlie offered to be my date. That was my first intimation that whatever we had was going to be serious. You don't spend twelve hours watching a movie genre you despise just to get laid (actually, I don't think anyone could possibly have the stamina to bone after watching movies from seven at night to seven in the morning). You only do that when you genuinely dig somebody and want her to be happy.

This does not mean that you should test the depth of your paramour's affection by suggesting dates you know she'll loathe. That's manipulative and douchey. Just be aware that someone who occasionally puts your happiness or convenience ahead of her own is probably someone who's planning to stick around awhile.

Finally, someone who *really likes you* thinks about your future together. This doesn't mean that after three dates she should be planning your wedding, naming your future kids, or buying a plane ticket to meet your mom, but if she's super into you, she'll start taking small steps to align her life with yours. If your lady friend is updating her pantry, her sporting equipment, her wardrobe, etc., so that she can spend more time with you—even if it's as simple as stocking up on sunscreen because you're outdoorsy, or buying a bus pass so she can visit you more often—she's probably open to the possibility of a future with you.

Keeping It Casual

On the other hand, you might not be looking for a future with anybody, and that's fine! Dating, smooching, and sleeping with cute people can be an end in itself, not just a way of holding auditions for the Last Person You'll Ever See Naked. If you want to have a casual relationship (or multiple casual relationships) instead of serious long-term monogamy, that's a perfectly valid choice, and don't let anyone tell you otherwise.

Bear in mind, however, that casual-dating or casual-sexing relationships are still relationships, and must be treated as such. You'll need to put at least a little bit of time and effort into maintaining them. People sometimes use "I'm not looking for a serious relationship" as an excuse to ride roughshod over the emotions of others, but you don't want to be that person. Not only is it bad for your karma, but lesbian gossip travels faster than the speed of light, and when you break one girl's heart you pretty much take a sledgehammer to your chances of ever banging any of her friends.

So when you're trying to date casually, be as honest, communicative, and respectful as possible. Disclose early that you're not looking for something monogamous or long-term;

it's never cool to mislead someone into thinking you want the same thing she does. Not even if she's super hot. Also, if you're dating multiple people and especially if you're sexing multiple people, you need to let all your partners know. For some people, the knowledge that you don't plan to be sexually exclusive will affect the safe-sex measures they want to take; for others, it will be the end of your relationship. That's totally fine—just move on to other prospects whose needs overlap more with your own. A big part of being an ethical casual dater is not pressuring anyone to do anything they're not comfortable with.

When you do find someone who's cute and fun and down to date without commitment, treat her well. Casual sex partners are not disposable and should not be disrespected just because you don't want to be girlfriends. Plus, a hookup that you're nice to is a hookup you might get to make out with again! Why would you want to jeopardize that?

Think of your dates and hookups as *friends*, albeit friends you sometimes see naked, not Sex People whose sole purpose in the universe is to provide you with sex. Be considerate of their feelings. Ask how their day was, and be supportive if it wasn't great. Don't hide them from your other friends or treat them like their presence in your life is shameful. It's fine to do the two a.m. post-bar booty call thing, but see them in the daylight once in a while, too. Occasionally spend time together doing things that don't involve orgasms; go bowling, play video games, whatever. Text them during the day if you hear a joke you know they'd love. These are not Designated Girlfriend-Only Activities—they're things you do with people you like.

Which brings us to the most important commandment of casual dating: Thou shalt not have sex with people you don't like. It's never worth it, no matter how long it's been since you got laid. Sleeping with someone you don't like or respect is a surefire way to feel sticky and greasy in your soul. (Remember that you can like and respect someone you don't know very well. This isn't about deep emotional intimacy; it's just about not being grossed out by their personality.) If there's no one you like and respect available, buy yourself a nice vibrator and don't get horizontal with anyone unless you can stand to hear them utter a complete sentence.

These Signals Don't Mix

One of the dating complaints I hear most often, in my advice in-box and in life, is "She's giving me mixed signals!" But when you break down the issue to its core components, you frequently—so frequently that "always" might be a more appropriate word—find that the signals being given are actually extremely clear.

In a typical case, let's-call-her-Amy and let's-call-her-Beth have been hanging out a lot, and Amy has a big crush. She wants to get girlfriended up, so one night at a party she asks Beth if she can kiss her, and they end up sexing in a mutual friend's bedroom. The next day, Beth tells Amy that she's not looking for a serious relationship right now, and Amy is heartbroken. But a week later, they hook up again. Amy emails me in a fever of confusion, wanting to know what the hell Beth's mixed signals mean.

The thing is, Beth is not giving Amy mixed signals at all.

She has been very clear about her desires: She likes Amy and wants to sleep with her, but she doesn't want to be her girlfriend.

Most of us have absorbed some degree of romantic conditioning from songs and television shows and cologne commercials and whatnot, and while many of these messages are harmful if not downright offensive, I often think the most pernicious one is the idea that all romantic or sexual attraction leads inexorably to True and Lasting Love. In truth, however, someone can enjoy spending time with you, think you're cute, and want to make out with your face without having any intention of becoming your significant other.

If you ask someone to date you and she says no, nothing she ever does after that counts as mixed signals, whether it's a flirty comment, a long hug, or hours of orgasms. There is simply no amount of oral sex that can transform a non-girlfriend into a girlfriend.

Don't drive yourself nuts trying to decipher someone's mixed signals when she's given you the only signal that really matters: saying she doesn't want to date you. If you're fine with no-strings hookups, feel free to pursue them, but when it comes to lasting romance, expend your energy on someone who hasn't already turned you down.

The Red Flag of Nuh-Uh

When you're dating, your goal is to find someone who's right for you, whether that means you're compatible for a night of carefree grinding, a few weeks of hanging out, or a lifetime of spooning and taking turns feeding the cat. You also have to keep an eye out for signs that someone is definitely *not* right for you, or what we in the advice-giving trade call "red flags." This term comes to us from the golden age of piracy, when ships would fly red flags to indicate that they had nothing on board worth plundering. (I made that up; I think it's actually from sports, but I like pirates more than sports.)

Even if you really dig someone, you should seriously consider bailing when you notice any of these classic bad signs. Anyone who displays them is usually miserable to be with in a serious relationship—no matter how good her cleavage looks in that top. There are always other tits in the sea. Err on the side of shaking her off before she has the chance to become your Nightmare Ex from Hell.

One of the biggest things to watch out for is a girl who hates all her exes. This doesn't mean she needs to be BFFs with everyone she's dated (although, in the lesbian world, it's a distinct possibility), but she should be able to get through a dinner date or two without chronicling all of their myriad character flaws. Someone who describes every girl she's ever kissed as "manipulative" or "psycho" or "clingy" is either pathologically unwilling to accept her share of blame or attracted to unhealthy relationships because she has some unresolved shit. Either way, she is a maelstrom of conflict and misery, and you want to avoid getting pulled under.

Run far away, too, from anyone your friends loathe. When you're attracted to someone, the sex hormones make your brain all weird (yes, this is highly technical terminology) and can convince you to overlook issues that would be a deal breaker if you were in a more settled frame of mind. But if your friends tell you they hate her, or if they say things like

"She seems really . . . I can tell that you're super into her!," you need to start developing an exit strategy. No one has ever shared a long and happy life with someone her friends couldn't stand. Your friends are smart and have great taste in people. That's why you're friends with them. Let their wisdom guide you.

Anyone who tries to persuade you to do something you don't want to do, especially early in the relationship, goes into the reject pile without delay. Yes, every relationship involves a certain amount of compromise, and you can't build lasting love by being completely inflexible, but neither can you build anything of value with someone who doesn't respect your boundaries. If your date tries to cajole you into sex or commitment after you say you're not interested, pump the brakes. No one who treats your comfort and safety like they're negotiable belongs in your bedroom or your life.

Hit the eject button on anyone with a scary temper. Violence and screaming are an automatic no-go, and even if she's not directing her overreactions your way, eventually she will. Don't date people who start bar fights, throw plates, or punch walls, and don't date people who yell at customer service workers for things that aren't their fault. Contrary to what pop culture sometimes tells you, none of those things make someone passionate or sexy. This also applies to anyone with an alcohol or substance abuse problem they're not seeking treatment for. You might think you're climbing on board a roller-coaster ride, but it's really more like a Tilt-A-Whirl that goes on for months or years until you're miserable and want to vomit but it never slows down enough for you to get off.

Oh, and don't date anyone who still lives with her ex. This one seems pretty self-explanatory.

Then there are the perfectly nice people—non-abusers, non-sociopaths—whom, for reasons that are neither their fault nor yours, you just shouldn't date. Don't date your boss or anyone who could be construed as your superior at your place of employment. Also, don't date anyone who is subordinate to you at work. It might be best to err on the side of never dating anyone whose paycheck comes from the same place as yours. A power imbalance in the workplace might seem totally irrelevant when the relationship is shiny and new, but if you fight or break up, working together can become nightmarish really quickly. It's all too easy for the higher-up person to make her subordinate ex's life hell without even meaning to.

Don't date anyone who's closeted or cheating. I don't care how gorgeous she is—if she has a boyfriend and he doesn't know about your standing weekly date to fuck each other silly in the backseat of your Prius, she is a bad investment. I understand that being closeted is really hard and deciding when to come out is a deeply personal decision, and I will never think less of anyone for waiting until later in life to do it, but getting into a relationship with someone who's going to hide your existence—not to mention a fundamental component of her identity—from her loved ones is signing up for a lot of unhappiness. And anyone who will cheat *with* you will also cheat *on* you. Fidelity is a character trait, not a prize you can earn by being the best girlfriend ever.

And don't date anyone who had a terrible breakup with your friend. In the queer community, "don't date exes" is not a hard-and-fast rule—honestly, it's barely a gentle suggestion. There aren't a lot of us to go around, and when you filter by age, geography, being able to do that thing you like with the ice cube, etc., the pool gets a lot smaller. You're definitely going to date a friend's ex at some point. (Hell, I married a friend's ex, and the friend in question gave a reading at our wedding.) It's cool. What's not cool is dating someone who genuinely made your friend miserable or broke her heart. When you do that, you're telling your friend, "My need to get laid is more important to me than your feelings!" If someone represents a major scar on your friend's soul, consider her out of bounds.

Handling Rejection

Everyone gets rejected. It is the most universal of all human experiences but somehow the most terrifying. We spend huge amounts of time and ridiculous quantities of energy trying to avoid it, because even though it's inevitable, it's devastating.

In the dating world, rejection lurks around every corner. Someone could decide "nope, not feeling it" when you ask her out, or after four dates, or two weeks before your wedding. I'm not trying to freak you out; I just want you to know what you're getting yourself into. Some people have the misguided idea, before they acquire much romantic experience, that if they can just manage to be the world's most perfect girlfriend, they can avoid ever having to go through the heart-crushing pain of rejection, but that is a total lie. You can do absolutely nothing wrong and still get kicked to the curb.

When someone you're really into tells you to hit the road, it will feel like you have failed, and the temptation to take it personally will be strong. I have thought some crazy things while in the grip of post-rejection misery, like "It's because my butt is too flat" or "This wouldn't have happened if I'd majored in history" or "Fuck it, that's it—I'm going to shave my head" (actually, that last one turned out to be a phenomenal idea). But the fact of the matter is, I'm a great person, and you probably are, too.

People don't reject you because they've drawn up a spreadsheet of your physical characteristics, personality traits, and life history and found too many flaws. They do it because they're just not feeling it—because you don't have chemistry. Chemistry isn't something you can create by trying, and lack of it isn't a failure on your part. When you get shot down, resist the urge to criticize yourself or embark on unnecessary self-improvement projects. You are not the problem. Even the smoothest, most conventionally attractive, and most romantically successful person you know has been rejected plenty of times—in fact, probably many more times than you, because you don't become smooth and romantically successful without putting in plenty of classroom hours in Getting Turned Down 101.

If you need to wallow for a little while after the hot girl from your yoga class says no to a brunch date, that's fine. When I was in ninth grade, my best friend asked a boy to a dance (we were liberated and empowered ladies, even back then), and he turned her down—an egregious breach of the social contract, as he had indicated in a note to a mutual friend that if she asked him, he would say yes. That day, she spent her lunch period hiding under a desk in an empty class-room, eating mint chocolate chip ice cream and crying. When lunch was over, she wiped her eyes and went about her day. This is still the most sensible approach to handling romantic disappointment I have ever seen.

Feeling crushed and hopeless when you get rejected is to-tally normal, and if you need to stay in for a weekend, drown-ing your sorrows in pizza and Netflix, do so with my blessing. But don't let the pain dissuade you from trying again. The more you face rejection, the less it throws you.

The Siren Song of Straight Girls

If you are a woman of the gay, bi, or queer persuasion, at some point in your romantic life you will almost certainly encounter that most pernicious of emotional pitfalls: crush-ing on a straight girl. I'm not talking about an "oh, she's cute; I'd totally be down if she was into girls" crush; I'm talking about the wholehearted, can't-sleep, can't-eat, can't-complete-a-sentence-in-her-presence debacle of totally inappropriate attraction. It can derail your life and your productivity with inescapable fantasies, and of course, if you're friends with the straight girl in question, it can make your friendship super weird, possibly forever. So you have that to look forward to!

When you find yourself plagued with an unrequited crush, it's tempting to try to create dream scenarios where you end up together, but this is a really bad idea. Fantasizing feeds the attachment, and what you need to do is starve it to death so that you can move on with your life, carefree and unencumbered. So, repeat after me, as many times as you need to until it really sinks in: My straight friend is not secretly in love with me.

Yes, I'm sure you know someone who went to high school with someone whose cousin was a straight girl who realized she was totally gaybones for her lesbian BFF and then they lived happily ever after, but I'm telling you, the odds in your favor are almost infinitely small. Whatever example you can think of exists only to get your hopes up and make you believe in a fairy tale. (I know that Lauren Morelli was married to a man when she fell in love with Samira Wiley. Rules do not apply to Samira Wiley. You are a lovely and talented person, but you are not Samira Wiley. Unless you are, in which case, *Holy shit, I love you, I can't believe you're reading my book, will you autograph it for me?*) Let go of the fantasy and walk it off. Otherwise, longing will fade into disappointment, disappointment will fester into resentment, and you'll be well on the way to ruining a perfectly good friendship.

Put away the photographs of you two together. Take a break from listening to the mix CD she made you and searching it for hidden clues of longing. Stop keeping your Saturday nights free of plans in case she calls. When she hugs you, remind yourself that people hug their platonic friends all the time. More than anything, when the urge to fantasize rises up inside you, crush it. Go for a walk, reorganize your bookshelf, make yourself an online dating profile—anything to keep your mind off the future you won't share with the girl you can't have. Find yourself someone to make out with, even if the two of you are wildly incompatible. Basically, the goal is to ignore your passion until it goes away—which, I promise you, it eventually will.

When to U-Haul

Yes, it's an offensive and belittling stereotype. "What do lesbians bring on a second date?" "A U-Haul!" Ha-ha-ha. Girls love commitment, so two girls must love it twice as much. Right? It's stupid, of course, but let's lean in real close so no one else can hear us, and I'll whisper, for your ears only, that it's actually . . . kind of . . . a little bit . . . true.

Okay, not for everyone. Maybe you're the type of queer girl who waits a long time to make sure everything's perfect before taking an enormous step like cohabitating. And that's cool! But for many of us, the nesting instinct is real. So how do you know when you're ready to wake up next to your ladylove every single day for the rest of your life, or at least for the rest of your lease?

Generally speaking, you shouldn't move in together until you've already had at least one big fight. You need to know that you and your girl are capable of working through conflict with mutual respect, open communication, and willingness to compromise, because I promise you, when you start living together, there will be conflict. If you genuinely believe that you're "just one of those couples who never fight," you are not ready to share a cable bill.

You also shouldn't move in together until you've had a few serious discussions about the future. I don't mean that you need to know where you're planning to send your children for preschool, but you should have at least a general idea of how you're each hoping the next year or two will go and how much your desires overlap. If she's planning to move to the mountains and grow organic tomatoes, and you're desperate to climb the ladder at your big-city job, living together may be more trouble than it's worth. And if you have no idea what she hopes her life will look like in a few months or years, you don't know each other well enough to U-Haul.

Then there are the smaller issues: Do you like each other's pets? Do your pets get along? If not, what will you do? (If the answer is "get rid of the unwanted pet," please stop reading my book, because we are no longer friends.) How similar are your standards of cleanliness? What about your expectations of privacy? You need to be able to answer all of these questions before you consider signing a rental agreement together.

And of course, moving in is never, ever a way of solving a problem in your relationship. If you've been fighting, getting an apartment together might seem like a novel way of distracting from your issues, but it is 1,000 percent guaranteed to cause more strife than it ameliorates. And never move in with your girlfriend just because you can afford a nicer place together than apart. The only reason to risk all the stress and challenges of moving in together is that you're totally in love and want to see each other every damn day. If that's not where you are, it's simply not worth it.

You Be You, Girl

When you're dating, it can be so easy to get swept up in the exhilaration and the infatuation and the eagerness to please. Sometimes it feels like dating is a competition, and the first one across the finish line (whether that means getting laid, moving in together, or having your third kid) wins . . .

something. So people go out of their way to make themselves extra sexy or extra agreeable or extra interested in college volleyball, because that's what the person they're currently dating wants, and there's intense pressure, both internal and external, to make relationships last at any cost.

But there are a couple of things to keep in mind. One, of course, is that a committed long-term relationship doesn't have to be your goal, now or ever. You don't have to pair-bond to have a fulfilling life, and your priorities are valid even if they don't include seeing the same person naked for the next five or twenty-five or sixty-five years.

Another is that even if lifelong love is something you want, you're looking for someone who is right for you, not just someone who happens to be around. It's never worth trying to squash yourself into a relationship that doesn't fit you. No matter how long it's been, no matter how much you want a partner, it's always better to be alone than to be unhappily coupled—and unhappily coupled is exactly where you'll end up if you're dishonest about who you are and what you want.

I know it sounds like a cheesy platitude, but it's real talk: Someone who is a good match for you will dig you exactly the way you are. She will be attracted to your body type and your intellect and your sense of humor and your passions and talents and quirks. To the right person, you will have no con column; everything she learns about you will only make her like you more. If finding out about your love of terrible puns kills her ardor, your relationship was never going to last to begin with.

Obviously, if there are aspects of yourself or of your life

you're unhappy with, it's worth putting effort into fixing them, because someone who's miserable and isn't taking steps to correct the situation can end up driving away even the people who love her dearly. But don't assume you have to mask your flaws in order to find true love. People way more [*whatever you think your worst quality is*] than you find love every day. Love isn't a prize that goes to the best or smartest or prettiest or most devoted. Love is a weird and inexplicable combination of hormones and luck and maybe some witchcraft or something, and every one of us is just stumbling around hoping to get lucky.

One time, I was throwing a party at my house, and my friend Penelope, a lesbian in her fifties, showed up sans girlfriend. It turned out they had broken up sometime in the last three hours. Penelope was totally unshaken by the split. "It just wasn't working," she said. "I'm too old to waste my time on someone who doesn't make me happy. The next one will be along soon."

It would not be an exaggeration to say that this totally changed my dating philosophy. I call it the Penelope Principle: If you're not happy, it's not worth your time—end of discussion. I've known people half Penelope's age who felt they had no option besides staying in their mediocre relationships forever because they were "too old" to start looking again, but honestly, no matter how old you are, you don't have time to mess around with someone who doesn't make your soul sing.

There are people out there who have what you need and need what you have, and if you keep looking, you're going to find them. But it's all the better if you're not already attached to someone who's a bad fit when the real deal comes along. Don't date someone you want to change, or someone who wants to change you. Just keep moving along until you find the person who's ready to appreciate the glorious, unique, weird, awesome little magic maker that you are.

Chapter 4

∞

But What Can Two Girls *Do*?: Your Guide to Queer Sex

Getting a date is only the tip of the iceberg when it comes to your love life. What do you do after the movie's over, when you're back at her apartment with the lights low and the expectations high? This chapter is for everything they didn't cover in your sex education class. Whether you're an experienced lady-lover or you've never even seen *yourself* naked, we'll talk about everything you need to know to have a satisfying, enjoyable, gloriously queer sex life.

Defining Sex

If you've been out as a queer chick for more than five minutes, you've probably encountered at least twelve variations on the eternally annoying question "How do two girls even have sex?" This is sometimes asked out of genuine (if inappropriate) curiosity, but more often you'll notice a derogatory undertone. The asker most likely doesn't really want an answer. What they're actually saying is, *Two women can't have sex. Sex requires a man.* (Or, *Sex requires a penis*, because people who make these kinds of statements aren't usually hip to the fact that genitals don't determine gender.)

Assuming you grew up on planet Earth, you were probably taught (via your sixth-grade health class, your parents, 99 percent of popular culture, etc.) that "sex" meant penis-in-vagina intercourse ending in male orgasm. Female orgasm was somewhere between optional and laughable, and other sex acts were either foreplay or unspeakably obscene. If this is your working definition of sex, it's not surprising that the idea of two women doing it might sound like a contradiction in terms.

But as you may already know from your own experimenting, two women absolutely can have mind-blowing sex (and also fun but kinda disappointing sex, and sex that doesn't rock your world but does bring you closer together emotionally, and pretty much every other kind, too). So if sex doesn't just mean "a cis guy and a cis girl going at it missionary-style until he comes," what *does* it mean?

Well, that's really up to you and your partner. You decide what constitutes sex based on what feels most enjoyable or intimate to you. For some people, it's not sex unless there's penetration. For others, it's not sex unless they get off. My personal sex/not sex border is hazy, but I pretty much count anything that could plausibly lead to an orgasm for either party.

"Sex" is a word that contains multitudes. When it comes to your own sex life, you decide what it means—both in terms of specific acts and in the larger context of your relationships.

But however you define sex, approaching it with curiosity, self-awareness, and respect for yourself and your partner make the difference between a lackluster sex life and one that's out of this world.

The First Time

The standard follow-up question to the above spiel goes something like this: "So, if sex can mean anything, how does a lesbian know when she's lost her virginity?" To which I usually respond, "That question is meaningless because virginity is an antiquated patriarchal concept that reduces a woman's worth to her sexual purity and is therefore irrelevant in an egalitarian society!" Not that I really think we live in an egalitarian society, but you know, be the change you wish to see and all that.

Even though the concept of virginity as something that you can "have" or "lose" (or, gag, "give" to someone, presumably so they can keep it in their scrapbook next to their prom pictures and concert tickets from bands they'll be embarrassed to have liked ten years from now) is kind of gross and demeaning, it's not unusual to feel a sense of anxiety or pressure before having sex for the first time. Trying something you've never done before can be intimidating, and pop culture leads us to believe that being "good" or "bad" at sex is a major determining factor in your value as a person.

The reality is twofold: One, your first few sexual experiences will almost undoubtedly be awkward. Sex is at least partially a physical skill, and no one is great at a physical skill the first time they try it. Be prepared for it to feel different than you expected (and different from masturbation), and allow for the possibility that you might not come on the first try. But two, awkward sex can still be good. If you're sharing it with someone you like and trust, sex that isn't multiorgasmically earthshaking can still be fun and worthwhile.

Any time you're considering having sex, but especially the first time, make sure your partner is someone to whom you feel safe expressing yourself. If you aren't comfortable saying "That feels weird—can you move your elbow?" or "I don't want to do that; let's try something else," you're not going to have good sex. And only have sex because you want to—that is, because you're attracted to the person you're with and want to express that attraction through mutually satisfying naked grinding—not because you're trying to prove that you love them, or because you don't want to be the last one of your friends to have sex, or whatever. Your first sexual experience will probably not quite live up to your expectations, but it's going to be a way bigger disappointment if you're not turned on by your partner.

Do what you can to make your early attempts at sex respectful and positive, but try not to romanticize your First Time too much. How satisfying and empowering was your first attempt to ride a bike? Probably not very. It was just a necessary step to take so that, later on, you could cruise with the wind in your hair and feel amazing.

Porn versus Reality

If you're an inexperienced lady-lover, you may have only encountered lesbian sex so far in porn. Most "lesbian" porn, however—like most porn in general—is produced for a presumed-male audience, so unless you're actively seeking out erotica produced by and starring queers, it's likely that what you've seen has, to put it generously, taken some artistic license with the lived reality of girl-on-girl action.

I want to tread carefully here, because sometimes the queer chick backlash against "lesbian" porn goes too far, and you end up with people saying, "No real lesbian would ever have sex like that!" Trust me on this one: Real lesbians have sex literally every way you can imagine and some you haven't thought of yet.

However, girl-on-girl porn tends to focus on how the act looks more than on how it feels, which is why you see a lot of vigorous, long-fingernailed thrusting without much else. Penetration is certainly a part of many queer women's sex lives, but it's not the only thing we do. Also, there's that weird thing in porn where a woman goes down on her partner from, like, two feet away; I understand that the viewer doesn't want an actress's face covering all the fun stuff, but in real life, the goal of oral sex is not to show off how far you can stick out your tongue.

Additionally, in mainstream porn, the women all tend to have the same body type: thin and white, with long hair and suspiciously gravity-defying, large breasts. There's nothing wrong, of course, with being a skinny white femme with a boob job, but there's nothing wrong with any other kind of body, either. Porn tends to either erase or grossly fetishize body types outside of its norm, but in real life, anything goes. No matter your shape, size, color, disability, age, or weird mole, someone out there is going to find you devastatingly sexy.

Basically, porn is all about the visual, and it promotes a seriously limited aesthetic standard. Real sex is about how it feels, to you and the person you're with. Sometimes the things that feel the best aren't the ones that would look the most titillating to an observer, but that doesn't mean you shouldn't pursue what turns you on. You don't have to try something (and you certainly don't have to like something) just because they do it in porn. You're not performing for anyone.

Safety First

It's a popular misconception that lesbian sex is inherently "safe" and can't result in unwanted pregnancies or STIs. Thus, lots of queer women are extremely lax with their safe-sex measures. Unfortunately, you absolutely can transmit infections and even (depending on the anatomy of your partner) get knocked up via girl-on-girl sex, so safer sex practices are still a necessity. (I'm using the phrase "safer sex" instead of the more common "safe sex" because there are no 100 percent risk-free sex acts. Unless you know with certainty that neither you nor your partner has anything transmissible, you can make your sex safer, but it's never guaranteed to be perfectly safe.) Know what your options are and be prepared to put them to use.

What constitutes "safer sex"? Basically, anything that prevents the exchange of fluids between you and your partner. If you have a hangnail or a paper cut on your finger and you put your finger in someone else's vagina, you can get any infection your partner has. If you have a cold sore on your lip and you perform oral sex on someone, you can give your partner genital herpes. If you use the same insertable sex toy with more than one person, you risk transmitting all manner of unpleasantness. While oral and manual sex pose a lower risk than penis-in-vagina penetration, lower risk doesn't mean no risk. If you're unsure of your partner's status or your own, or if either of you has an STI, you should use dental dams, latex gloves, and condoms to minimize the possibility of transmission. (Anything even vaguely phallic in shape can wear a condom; they're not exclusive to flesh-and-blood penises.)

Actually, latex gloves and other barrier methods are great to have around even when you and your partner are both STI-free. Vaginal discharge is acidic, and allowing it to come into contact with even a minor hangnail is an easy way to bring the mood from sexy to "ow, ow, goddamn ow!" in three seconds or less.

Also, when you're thinking about safety, it's always worth remembering that "queer lady sex" doesn't necessarily mean "sex with two vaginas." Lesbians come in all shapes and genital configurations, and yes, some queer women have penises. If that's you or your partner, remember that P-in-V and P-in-A sex carry a higher risk of transmission than oral or manual, so it's even more important to use a condom if there's a chance either of you has something communicable. If you and your partner are reproductively compatible, you should also be discussing whether pregnancy is a desirable outcome and, if not, what you'll do to prevent it. (Hormone replacement therapy for trans women decreases fertility, but always check with a doctor to make sure it's safe before having unprotected P-in-V.)

Try not to think of safer sex as a buzzkill or a distraction;

saying "Hey, let's grab a dental dam" doesn't need to break the mood any more than saying "Hold on, my wrist is cramping." Protecting your sexual health and that of your partner should be a shared goal, not something you have to talk someone into. If you find that negotiating your safer sex decisions is detracting from the overall experience, the problem isn't that safety is unsexy; the problem is that you're banging an inconsiderate jerk. Move on to greener pastures.

Yes-or-No Questions

You really can't have a complete discussion of sex and the ethics thereof without talking about consent. Though the majority of perpetrators of sexual assault are men, rape committed by and between queer women does exist, and it's important to be aware of it and take steps to prevent it.

Never, ever, under any circumstances, do anything sexual to or with another person without first obtaining that person's consent. While "no means no" is still the law in most places, your personal standard should be "yes means yes"— that is, nothing other than a clear and enthusiastic affirmation of consent gives you permission to keep going. Being unconscious or incapacitated by drugs or alcohol also means no. Pulling away means no; being unresponsive means no. "I don't know" means no. "Maybe" means no—or at the very least, slow way down and talk about it before continuing. If you're not sure, assume you do not have consent. The worst-case scenario of interpreting consent as nonconsent is that you don't get laid when you could have, and I promise you, there will be other opportunities. The worst-case scenario of interpreting nonconsent as consent is rape.

Making sure you have consent is even more necessary than making sure you're having safer sex, and just like safer sex, there's no reason to view it as distracting or libido-killing. Questions like "Can I touch you here?" and "Do you want me to go down on you?" are a totally normal—and hot—part of a good sexual encounter. It's not enough to just ask "Do you want to have sex?" because that can include a vast array of activities, some of which your partner might want and some of which she might not. If she says yes to oral sex, you still have to ask before fucking her with a strap-on. This remains true even if you've been in a relationship for years.

It is the sole and unequivocal responsibility of every human being to avoid committing sexual assault; the onus is never on the potential victim to "protect" herself from being assaulted. That said, it's always a good idea to distance yourself from people who don't respect your boundaries. Someone who tries to talk you into one more drink when you've already said you have to get up early tomorrow will probably also try to override your preferences when it matters a lot more. Stay away from folks who don't seem to hear it when you say "no," or who take "maybe" as "yes." Those people are unworthy of your company.

What Makes It Good?

Everyone wants to be good at sex, but there are about as many definitions of "good sex" as there are people in the human race. Being a legendary lay isn't a question of mastering certain specific physical skills or complicated techniques; it's about being communicative, receptive, and willing to work with your partner to make the experience the best it can possibly be for the two of you.

There are, when you get down to it, only a couple of basic sexual activities, with nearly infinite variations based on the anatomy and preferences of the people involved. Pretty much every sex act consists of either penetration (fingering, strap-on sex, P-in-V, P-in-A, fisting) or rubbing (cunnilingus, vibrators, scissoring). So the only moves you really need are "in and out" and "back and forth." Sure, those moves will go more smoothly once you've had a little bit of practice and learned that that cramp in your wrist will go away if you just work through it, but by minute five of your first sexual experience you'll be about as technically "good" at it as you're ever gonna get.

Good sexual partners do not have preternatural G-spot-finding abilities or fancier sex toys than you do. What they have is attention to and respect for the people they're fucking. They check in to make sure what they're doing feels good, and if it doesn't, they adjust accordingly. They don't do something because they assume they're supposed to, but because the person they're with has expressed a genuine desire for it. They don't put pressure on their partners to try things they're not comfortable with.

Good sexual partners communicate openly about their own desires. They say "I want . . ." and "Will you please . . ." because they know that the best sex happens when both (or all) the people involved are having a great time. They may not have a totally flawless body image, but they're able to transcend their self-consciousness and get down to the fun and weird and sweaty and passionate work of sex without worrying too much about what they look like. Good sex partners encourage their lovers to ask for what they want, but feel confident saying no when they're not interested or don't think they can stretch that way. They also remember that real-life sex is often silly, despite what you see in the movies, and that just because someone sneezes or elbows you in the ribs or giggles or rolls off the bed doesn't mean the night (or morning or lunch break) is ruined.

And the best sexual partners know that "good" is subjective, and that compatibility matters more than raw physical prowess. If you like sex that's slow and romantic and intense with tons of eye contact, you are not going to have good sex with someone whose goal is a fast, rough, athletic encounter and who scores her fucks based on how many bruises she has afterward. No matter how much you like each other or how gorgeous she is, if you have fundamentally different sexual tastes, it's unlikely you'll be able to have sex that's incredible for you both.

Being a good lover isn't something you accomplish through a rigorous training montage. It comes from knowing your own desires, being honest about them, and being willing to communicate—and having a partner who does the same. You might not be world-class on your first try, but practice and just generally being a cool and respectful person will get you where you want to go.

Dirty Talk

Have I mentioned enough times the absolutely indispensable necessity of *talking about sex*? It is so key, and yet so tragically underrepresented in contemporary media. Nearly every sex scene in books and movies and TV takes place in almost total silence, aside from some mood music and maybe a little gasping. This would be a fine precedent to set if every person alive enjoyed the exact same sex acts in the exact same order, but since that's not the case, the only way to make sure you're having sex that's awesome for both you and your partner is to use your words.

Being a good sexual communicator is a skill that can take years to develop, but it starts with knowing what you want and being confident that what you want is valid. Many of us internalize the version of sex that we see in Hollywood or porn as the only correct way to bang, so if we want something different, we think it's weird and embarrassing and we lie about it. We go through the motions we think are expected of us and never work up the courage to say "Actually, I'm not that into penetration, but I'd love to scissor with you." It's almost impossible to get good at dirty talk when you can't be honest about what you really like.

So start by paying attention to your desires—what you fantasize about, what you need in order to have an orgasm. If you don't know, spend some time getting to know your body. Masturbate. Read erotica. Make a mental note of what gets you amped up and what sends you over the edge. Once you know what you're into, practice saying it to yourself, in your head or out loud. Actually form it into sentences: "I need a lot of focus on my clit." "I'm really turned on by the idea of wearing a strap-on." Being honest and specific with yourself about what you dig will help you be more open with your partners.

Then, when you're in bed (or in a shower or tent or whatever) with that sexy someone, start with what you've practiced. It's usually best to focus on what you want—"It would be so hot if you'd get on top"—rather than what you don't want—"I don't like this position." Telling someone what not to do can result in a coitus interruption while they ask follow-up questions to figure out what you'd prefer. If you need a pause, that's totally fine, but if you want to keep going, aim for constructive criticism. Being told that you're doing something wrong can be a turnoff, but being told how to do it better is hot. Instead of "Not so fast," say "Go slower."

Dirty talk is a great way of maintaining communication with your partner, making sure you both know what's working and what's not, and affirming ongoing consent throughout your bone-fest, but it can also be a huge turn-on for its own sake. Telling your partner that you love what she's doing isn't just communicating useful information; it's really sexy.

If you're a talker, make sure you and your partner are on the same page regarding appropriate vocabulary. Some people like to use pet names during sex; others find them totally boner-killing. Your favorite synonym for oral sex might send your partner into uncontrollable giggles. I am still not over the convulsion of horror I felt the time someone used the phrase "making love" while we were fucking. It's a little meta, but if you communicate about the best way to communicate, you'll be well on your way to the uninhibited sex of your dreams.

Scissor Me Like a Hurricane

Scissoring is, without a doubt, the sex act that has caused the most controversy and strife in the lesbian community. If you want to start a brawl in a dyke bar, you can spend weeks sleeping with everyone's girlfriends or you can skip all the preamble and just ask, "So, what does everyone think about scissoring?"

For those not yet in the know, scissoring is when two people with vulvas grind them together for sexy reasons, interlocking their legs like a couple of pairs of scissors (I guess? I'm not sure why you would ever do this with actual scissors; nomenclature is a mystery). If you're into it, it can be intimate, fun, and really hot. If it doesn't work for you, however, it may seem like a bizarre yoga pose with no real point.

I will admit that I personally belong to the latter camp. Until and unless I find a partner with a prehensile clitoris, scissoring is just not quite focused enough to get me there. That said, I prefer to take a live-and-let-live approach to sexual positions that don't appeal to me, and I encourage you to do the same. If you're sensitive enough to get off while scissoring—or if you're not, but you like it anyway, because sex doesn't always have to lead directly to orgasms—rock on with your bad self and ignore the naysayers.

Queer women who are anti-scissoring evangelists tend to

talk about it the same way many of us talk about so-called lesbian porn: as something that was invented to pander to the male gaze rather than to satisfy actual women. I can understand this point of view because I used to feel this way myself. To someone who's tried scissoring without much success, it sounds almost like a douchey straight-dude joke: "What can two girls do, rub their vaginas together? Ha-ha! Up top! Hand me another Budweiser, Chad!"

But once again, it's vitally important to remember that everyone has different needs and wants, and the thing that rocks your world in bed might be totally yawn-worthy to someone else. It's a big, beautiful, queer-ass world out there, and scissoring is just as valid as the hundreds of other ways two or more ladies can get down with each other. Don't police other people's sex lives! (Unless you're partners and have a cop fetish in which you are consensually participating.)

Also, if you've been trying and trying but scissoring just isn't working for you, sliding a bullet vibrator in between your clits is kind of cheating, but it definitely makes things a *lot* more exciting.

Kiss with a Fist

To some people, fisting might sound weird, unpleasant, or downright scary, but if you're someone who enjoys intense penetration, it can be more fun than just about anything else.

Fisting means putting your entire hand into your partner's vagina, or, more challenging and less common, their anus. It's usually not a first-date activity, nor is it something you'll want to try before you have a fair amount of sexual experience under your belt. You need to be very comfortable with and aware of your body, and able to communicate with your partner, in order to fist happily and safely.

It's always good to have a bottle of lube within arm's reach, because ideally you'll work up to fisting slowly over a period of time, and stopping the sex to go digging through your toy box kind of throws off the groove. Also, because of all the lube, you'll probably want to slide a towel under your partner's hips (or your own, if you're the one getting fisted). Otherwise you're gonna have to get up afterward and wash the sheets, which can really kill the afterglow.

As with anything physically strenuous, you'll need to warm your partner up first, so start with some gentle finger-banging to get her relaxed and in the mood. Gradually add more fingers as you go. When your partner's ready, you want to curl your fingers into a kind of tube, with your thumb in the middle, keeping your hand at its narrowest possible diameter as you slide in. You don't actually make a fist until your hand is fully inside your partner, unless she's super keen to find out what childbirth would feel like in reverse.

The secret to successful fisting is going really slowly, using plenty of lube, and checking in verbally pretty much the whole time: "Is this good? Should I push? Do you need a second?" If your partner (the fistee) tenses up or says "ow" or makes an unhappy face, you (the fister) should stop immediately and wait for further information. What you should *not* do is yank your hand back. Any sudden movements will be way too intense for your partner, so always go slow and smooth unless specifically instructed otherwise. Sometimes it's best to hold your hand perfectly still while the fistee pushes with her hips, so that she can have total control over the speed and pressure. Once the hand is all the way inside, a tiny bit of motion will have a huge effect, so keep your gestures minimal and controlled until encouraged to speed up.

Fisting can be hot, but it is absolutely not mandatory! It's always okay to say "Ow, stop" or "This isn't going to work tonight" or "This isn't going to work ever." You don't ever have to prove yourself or impress your lover by pushing past your comfort level and potentially hurting yourself. Some of us are always going to be three-finger gals, and that's perfectly okay.

Fingernails

There are a lot of you out there worrying about whether your fingernails are helping or hurting your odds of getting laid. I know, because I hear from you regularly. So let's chat.

Conventional wisdom and that one episode of *The L Word* would have you believe that all queer women have short fingernails and that's how you can tell us apart from the straight girls. As a result, some queer femmes who love their French-manicured claws are having a crisis of confidence. Darlings, let me take you by the hands (your hands look great, by the way; that color is so perfect on you) and reassure you that it doesn't make a damn bit of difference.

First of all, maybe, like, three people have ever refused to fuck someone because of their fingernails. Have you seen what straight men's paws look like? Yikes. And yet women still sleep with them! It's fine.

Second, you can totally finger-bang with slightly overgrown nails without any adverse effects for your partner. As long as they don't extend past the tip of your finger, they're unlikely to do any damage. You should, however, make sure they're always super clean and filed into smooth ovals with no sharp or ragged edges. If it could snag on your tights, it could snag somewhere way less pleasant. I don't care how butch or uninterested in personal grooming you are; make friends with your emery board.

Third, there's a way to have great manual sex even with inch-long press-ons! Some incredibly helpful soul shared it in a comment thread on one of my columns back in the day, and I wish I knew her name and how to contact her with my profound thanks. The way it works is, you stick a cotton ball in each fingertip of a latex glove, put the glove on your hand, and go to town. Voilà—instant fun for you and your lover, who's no longer in danger of receiving internal lacerations!

Let your heart be your guide to fingernail length. Just keep them squeaky clean and never get one of those manicures with rhinestones or anything else that could fall off inside another person's body, and you'll be cool. And if you're crushing on a girl with incredible long nails, don't assume that means she isn't queer, but go forward with courage in your heart and latex gloves in your purse.

Hair and There

The only body-image question that has queer girls more twisted up with worry than the fingernails issue is "What should I do with my pubic hair?" Of course, the short answer—as with anything pertaining to how you should groom and style your own personal flesh vehicle—is, "Do whatever you want." But there's a little more to it than that. (Which should be the unofficial tagline of queer women everywhere, don't you think? "No, I'm not mad that she had lunch with her ex, but there's a little more to it than that.")

As strongly as I feel that your intimate landscaping should be a question for you and no one else, except maybe your waxer if the spirit is willing and the wallet is full, there's no denying that pubic hair—and the lack thereof—carries political implications. If I remove it, am I declaring allegiance to heteropatriarchal beauty standards that demean and infantilize women? If I don't, am I perpetuating stereotypes about queer women and rendering myself aggressively unfuckable? If I try for some kind of middle ground, will I succeed only in annoying people on both sides? How can I be sure that the first time I get pantsless with someone, she won't think I'm weird?

Queer girls are somewhat less susceptible to the vagaries of male-gaze-directed beauty standards than our straight sisters, but that doesn't mean that the current trend toward total hairlessness hasn't infiltrated our community to some extent. Still, it's far from mandatory. Anecdotally, it seems to me that more of us prefer to do a little trimming or edging, or just put on the *Frozen* soundtrack and Let It Grow. So if you don't feel like devoting time, energy, and/or money toward crotchal deforestation, you're in good company—but you're also not alone if you prefer to go bare.

Though porn and Hollywood tend to portray naked female bodies according to one very specific set of aesthetic guidelines, in real life what distinguishes you from the airbrushed magazine-cover beauty standard is exactly what makes you hot, unique, and desirable. Whether you have a neatly groomed bush, a wild garden, or a little bit of razor burn (sensitive skin that's had hair removed is seldom as smooth as *Playboy* would have you believe), someone who's into you is going to find it irresistible. I have never in my life had a potential sexual partner reject me because of my ladyscaping choices, and I don't know anyone else who has, either.

I also occasionally hear from women who are contemplating their sexual debut, wondering if the pubic hair of their future partners will end up being a deal breaker. If this is a concern you share, I want to reassure you that if you're turned on by someone, and they reciprocate the feeling to the point of nakedness, almost nothing can get in the way. The idea of pubic hair might be off-putting, but the reality—pubic hair in context, attached to a sexy person who is into you— will probably turn out to be fine. (Also, yes, it will get in your mouth. This is not as big a deal as you might imagine. Just say "Hold on a sec," pull it out, and go back to what you were doing.)

Whatever your personal predilections, there is only one hard-and-fast rule: Never demand that the person you're banging change her grooming habits to suit your preferences. This is an unacceptable request, and everyone who makes it goes directly to Lesbian Hell, where you have to watch Tara from *Buffy the Vampire Slayer* get shot over and over for eternity.

Babes in Toyland

Remember the feeling you used to have as a kid, meandering through the aisles of a seemingly never-ending toy store, overwhelmed and overjoyed by the possibilities? It doesn't have to disappear when you grow up—you can replicate it by going sex toy shopping! (Along with, unfortunately, the subtle but inescapable ennui that creeps in after playing with your new toy for a few minutes and realizing that you probably could have picked something better.)

Sex toys (or sex tools, as one of my friends likes to call them) are an optional addition to your naked repertoire, but honestly, why would you want to opt out? Lots of people still think of sex shops as sleazy or gross, but many of them today are totally clean and reputable, and have respectful, well-trained staff. It's always fun—and educational—to spend an hour or two wandering the aisles of your local independent, woman-owned sex shop alone or with your partner.

Although browsing without a clear goal in mind can be great, it's useful to have some idea of what you're looking for, so you don't get completely distracted and baffled by the array of choices. Are you looking for a strap-on? Do you want accessories to help you try out bondage? Organic lube? Think about the kind of sex you're having and the kind you'd like to have, and go in with a plan, even if it's a vague one (though impulse buying is okay, too). Vibrating toys are a great place to start, as they can be incorporated into almost any sex act or position to intensify things for one or both partners. For instance, if you like vaginal penetration but can't come from it,

a vibrating cock ring will take your P-in-V or strap-on sex to
a whole new level.

If you haven't used sex toys before, start simple. Don't
blow big money on an enormous, rechargeable, vibrating,
double-ended dildo before you've ever had strap-on sex.
Won't you be heartbroken if you try it and realize that you
can't quite get the angle right and you have this useless two-
hundred-dollar item that you definitely cannot return? Your
first time out, get a fairly small and inexpensive version of the
toy you want, to determine whether it's worth the cost of an
upgrade. It's also a great idea to chat with the employees
about what you're looking for (you don't need to be embarrassed about shopping for sex paraphernalia; every single
customer they interact with is doing the exact same thing).
They'll be able to tell you which features you might actually
want and which ones are just bells and whistles slapped on as
an excuse to charge more. Don't assume that the fanciest toy
is always the best one. I've spent a lot of money on sex toys in
the years since my then-roommate got me a gift certificate to
Fascinations for my eighteenth birthday, but if I were stranded
on a desert island and could bring only one thing, I'd want it
to be the most basic, no-fuss vibrator I own.

Make sure to keep your sex toys clean (different materi-
als require different cleaning products, so check the packag-
ing before you wash), and carefully put them away. If you use
rechargeables, keep them charged; if you prefer battery-
operated, keep batteries on hand at all times. Nothing kills a
moment like the sputtering out of a dead sex toy. Have a designated place to keep your toys where unsuspecting roommates or houseguests aren't likely to stumble across them;

owning sex toys isn't anything to be embarrassed about, but generally speaking, people who aren't fucking you don't want to know what brand of butt plug you prefer. Store lube upright so it doesn't leak and make things sticky.

Sterilizing your sex toys between uses, and especially between partners, is crucial to safer sex. Some people believe you should dispose of your sex toys after a breakup, because it's somehow inappropriate to use the same handcuffs with your new girlfriend that you used with your ex. I don't see the point of that—do you buy a new bed every time you find a new person to share it with?—but if you prefer to rebuild your collection with each new ladylove, or if you just have a bunch of toys lying around that you don't use anymore, you can recycle your old vibrators, dildos, etc. It's good for the earth and thus your sexual karma. Check out sextoyrecycling .com for more information.

Think Kink

Very broadly defined, kinky sex is anything that deviates from conventional sex acts. This is, of course, an almost useless definition, because it's so difficult to determine what counts as "conventional" sex in the first place. I don't have the time, the energy, or the breadth of knowledge to list, much less explain, every potential sexual kink, but let's say this: If you hesitate to bring it up with a new sex partner because you're afraid they won't be into it, it probably counts as a kink.

There's an odd correlation drawn in pop culture between kinkiness and sex drive—an assumption that kinky people are promiscuous and promiscuous people are kinky, linked to the erroneous belief that kink is somehow *more sexual* than "normal" sex. According to this train of thought, the more sex you have, the weirder sex you want. Let's nip this idea in the bud right now. You can have unorthodox sexual preferences and a low libido; you can be a ravening sex fiend who never does anything but enjoy cunnilingus, then finger-bang, then fall asleep. Kink is not a level of sex that you'll one day work up to. Like sexual orientation, being kinky seems to be mostly innate and only occasionally influenced by experience.

This means that if you have a particular kink, you're unlikely to "outgrow it" or "get over it." Your particular preferences will probably always be a facet of your sexual identity, and the best thing you can do is get comfortable with them. This may involve finding a partner whose tastes match yours, or someone with a different kink who doesn't mind tying you up on Tuesdays if you'll dress up as Batgirl on Thursdays. It might also mean forgoing your kink in real life because your partner's not into it, and thinking about it instead when you're having quality time with your Hitachi. Relationships always involve trade-offs, and only you can decide whether a particular sacrifice is worth it.

If you want to meet people who share your kink (or other kinky people in general), there are kinky social media sites, the largest being FetLife. Most major cities also have a real-life kinky social scene; Google will help you find it. A good place to start would be searching "[*name of your city*] + munch." A munch is a gathering of kinky people for socializing purposes, where no actual sex acts will take place, and it's a good way to dip a toe into the scene. Getting involved with a kinky community is a good way to learn about ethical kink (which stresses never engaging in anything sexual with someone who does not or cannot consent, having safe words, and being aware of and communicating about risks) and a safe way to discover new weird-sex skills. You can also, of course, practice kink in the privacy of your own home and never share the details with anyone you're not actively boning, but being kinky isn't necessarily some deep, dark secret that you must never tell a soul. The choice is yours!

If you're a kinky gal with a vanilla (or non-kinky) partner, or a vanilla gal with a kinky partner, it's important to remember that sexual preferences are value-neutral. Someone being less kinky than you doesn't mean she's closed-minded or boring; someone being kinkier doesn't mean she's depraved or slutty. Being sexually incompatible, and even deciding to end a relationship because of it, is okay. Trying to shame or coerce someone into having sex that she's not interested in—that's way less cool. If she's not into it and you can't live without it, it's time to go your separate ways.

Sex and the Trans Girl

If you're a woman who's into women, you can have queer sex—no matter your genitals or gender history. You can even have P-in-V, and it's still queer sex! Please feel free to ignore and/or defenestrate anyone who tells you otherwise.

It's not unusual for trans people to have more-complicated-than-average relationships with their bodies (not that anyone's body image is simple, Jesus no), and thus, solid communication skills are paramount. If you are trans and not generally or publicly out, it's probably a good idea to let your date/partner/bone-friend know before you get down to sexy times—not because you "owe" them that information or because you're deceiving them by withholding it, but because it should cue them to be more sensitive and aware of your boundaries. Plus, if someone is going to be shitty about your identity, it's better to find out that they're not good enough for you before you sleep with them.

Just like cis people, trans people's sexual preferences cover a vast span of orientations and activities; the possibilities are limitless. According to Dylan Ley (my queer trans Twitter friend whom you met in Chapter 2), "Sex as a trans woman can be terrific; just leave your assumptions at the door, and figure out how to make it great." Dylan also points out that while everyone's desires are subject to change over time, hormone replacement therapy can result in quicker or more drastic shifts, so ongoing communication and checking in, both with your partner and within yourself, are crucial.

If you're a cis lady with a trans ladylove, again, Dylan advises communication, honesty, and not making assumptions. "Google is your friend, but also don't expect everything you read to apply to your lady." Be sure to check in with her—and scrupulously respect her boundaries—regarding what parts of her body are okay to touch, and what words she wants you to use when referring to them.

More than anything, remember that who you are and what you want (sexually, romantically, for lunch, whatever) is totally okay. I concur with Dylan, who wants you "not to settle for people who make you feel guilty about your identity, like they are a saint for dating you. Even if opportunities for dating seem scarce, crappy partners are not worth the energy they consume. You are good, valuable, and worth dating for who you are." Keeping that in mind, go forth and get your boink on.

Lust Long Distance

There are lots of challenges that you face when you date someone who lives far away—loneliness, insecurity, falling behind on your favorite TV shows because you're waiting to watch them together—but one of the biggest hurdles is going unsexed for as long as it takes to save up for a plane ticket. In ancient times, long-distance girlfriends had nothing to get them through the day but the occasional sexy letter featuring, perhaps, a demure pencil sketch with a hint of boob (I'm not really up on my historical erotica, but that sounds about right). Today, however, you can take advantage of the myriad opportunities technology offers to assuage your geographically inconvenient lady cravings.

Phone sex sometimes gets a bad rap, but when you can't have your girl beside you in the flesh, her voice in your ear is the next best thing. This is when you really put the dirty talk skills we discussed earlier in the chapter to work. You know all those things you've been wishing to do together, if only she were here? Tell her about them, in detail. For bonus points, go shopping (together or separately) and buy the same brand of vibrator to use during your phone dates. It's the R-rated version of "we're both looking up at the same moon." The occasional naked Skype session doesn't hurt, either.

If you don't have enough privacy for phone or Skype sex, sexting is a great plan B. In fact, for any couple that doesn't get a lot of face-to-face time, the occasional dirty text during the day is a nice way to check in and let her know you're thinking about her . . . and about how great her butt looks when she wears high heels. To begin a sexting session, all you have to do is send her those four little words: "I'm thinking about you." She will almost invariably respond, "What are you thinking?" and you can take that opportunity to respond in as romantic or filthy a manner as you see fit. This is also a good way to stay connected if you're on wildly different schedules and need to fit your sexy activities into the five minutes between her waking up and your going to bed.

Sending risqué pictures is always a fun way to bridge the gap—although, ugh, I hate that I even have to say this, but if you have nude shots where you're identifiable, make sure they're really well protected, and don't send them to anyone you don't trust. Likewise, if your lady sends you something scandalous, don't show it to anyone, no matter how much you want to prove that you really do have a girlfriend in Canada and her tits are every bit as great as you've always said. And don't leave your phone on the bus.

Finally—old-school as it is—there's nothing quite like getting an actual letter, ink on paper, with your name on it and a plethora of sweet (or dirty) nothings inside. Think of it as writing you-and-your-girlfriend fan fiction and go wild. For a little something extra, plant a lipstick kiss on the page or spritz it with your cologne to give her a vivid sense memory of how freaking great you are.

Good Girlfriend, Lousy Lay

Sometimes, even when two people love each other very, very much, they still cannot make it work when the pants come off. This is one of the greatest tragedies in life, but it is also more or less unavoidable. At some point, you will care about someone greatly, but try as you might, the sexual chemistry just won't be there.

Sometimes this can be overcome with communication and a willingness to accommodate. Talking through what you want and what you're willing to do can be a great bonding experience, but it can also help you connect in more . . . vital ways. You might not be into the idea of spanking in general, but realizing how much it turns your girlfriend on can make it seem way more appealing. Compromise, if it comes from a place of joy and a mutual desire to provide each other with totally rockin' orgasms, can be a magical relationship-saver.

On the other hand, sometimes you just can't compromise, and that's okay, too. It is never, ever your responsibility to participate in sex that you don't like or don't want in order to keep your partner happy. It is never selfish to say no. At the same time, it's imperative to respect your partner's no, and to never try to cajole her into doing something she doesn't want to do.

Sexual incompatibility matters as much as you think it does. If you can have a totally happy and fulfilling relationship with mediocre or infrequent sex, that's great. If you can't, it's okay to say so. Some people will accuse you of being shallow if you leave an otherwise wonderful partner over bad sex, but if getting well and regularly laid is an important component of your happiness, there's nothing shallow about prioritizing it. Staying in a relationship where you're slowly going crazy for want of a really good fuck will only lead to resentment and more heartache for you both in the long run. Likewise, gritting your teeth through sex you're not into is not a recipe for lasting romance.

Listen to your heart, but also listen to your junk. If one or both are saying "run for the hills," don't waste time wondering what someone else would think of your reasons. You deserve not just a great love, but a great lover. Don't settle for less.

Chapter 5

∞

A Queer Chick's Guide to Heartbreak

So you've perfected your coming-out speech, you know where all the cool gay and bi ladies hang out in your hometown and in the surrounding suburbs, and you can go from zero to girlfriend in under thirty seconds. Sadly, you're still just a novice queer chick until you've been through a couple of world-ending, heart-stomping breakups. It happens to everyone—just keep your chin up, take deep breaths, and crank some Queen. You'll get through it and live to process another day. This chapter is your breakup survival kit.

Know When to Fold 'Em

In some ways, the easiest breakups are the ones that arrive already gift-wrapped for you—the ones where your sweetie is the one to say "I don't think this is working out. Can you have your side of the closet empty by tonight so that

Lauren can start moving in?" Obviously, those breakups still destroy you emotionally and leave you a desolate shell of a human being who can never trust again, and we'll talk about that in a minute, but at least you don't have to be the one who makes the decision.

Taking the initiative to pronounce your relationship dead is a whole different, far more terrifying ball game. Sure, there are the easy decisions, like when she cheats on you so egregiously that you can't possibly forgive her. But most breakups aren't like that. Mostly, people don't hurt each other that terribly or dramatically—or, when they do, it's after such a long, slow buildup of unhappiness that it barely feels out of the ordinary. You need to learn how to discern when a good relationship has gone bad (or when it was never good to start with), so you can make a graceful exit and start moving toward your happier, healthier existence.

It's important to remember that although being happily coupled and happily single are equally valid, being single and unhappy about it is *way* better than being in an unhappy relationship. No matter how afraid you are of being alone or how much you want to share your life with someone, it's not worth sticking it out with a love that's mostly dead, held together by routine and inertia. When you're in a terrible relationship, all your options seem to dry up and disappear, and your world shrinks and warps. Everything starts to feel empty and hopeless. But when you're alone, even if you'd rather not be, you have options. You can get to know yourself and figure out what you really want, rather than roll with something you've convinced yourself is good enough.

If you're wondering whether it's time to leave your relationship, it almost definitely is. Whatever logistical questions stand in your way—can you afford to live alone? Will your parents be disappointed? Will your kids be heartbroken?—you can and must overcome them. It's better to live in a crappy, run-down house with six roommates than to share a mansion with someone who makes you miserable. Your parents will get over it. Your kids are better off growing up with separated, happy parents than with coupled parents who can barely tolerate each other. Whatever is keeping you where you are, unless it's a deep and all-consuming desire to share your life with this specific person in all her glorious strengths and flaws and passions and idiosyncrasies, it's not enough. You can get past it. You can find the courage to go.

Here are a few hard-and-fast rules for breaking up: Don't stay with someone who hurts you physically or emotionally. Don't stay with someone who makes you feel unworthy. Don't stay with someone who makes you feel boring or unattractive, and don't stay with someone you find boring or unattractive. Don't stay with someone who's unfaithful to you, however the two of you define faithfulness. Don't stay with someone you're embarrassed to introduce to your friends. Don't stay with someone who tells you that she's the best you can do. Don't stay with someone who wants you to give up your friends or the things you love. Don't stay with someone who doesn't want you to achieve your dreams. Don't stay with someone who makes you feel that you have to earn her love. Don't stay with someone because you believe you can save her from herself. Don't stay with someone because it will hurt her if you leave. Trust me: In the end, staying together when you don't love her back will hurt her so much more.

And this is the big one: Don't stay with someone just because you love her. Love is not always enough. Your relationship should give you more than it costs you. It should make you happy more than it makes you sad. All relationships require some compromise, but in good compromises, what you win is more valuable than what you lose. If you find yourself constantly telling your friends that "love takes hard work" and "relationships aren't easy," that's a red flag. In a good relationship, most of the work that goes into nurturing your love and keeping it alive doesn't feel like work; it feels worthy and necessary. It's caring for something you love—like tending to your garden, or practicing your scales, or stretching a sore muscle—not desperately trying to stave off a crisis. If you're constantly in crisis mode, this is not the right love for you.

When you know you want to leave, start figuring out how you're going to do it. Don't wait around to see if you change your mind. You're not going to change your mind; you're just going to cause yourself and your partner a lot more misery by dragging things out. And don't, for the love of Queen Latifah, be the person who doesn't have the guts to say you want to break up, so you start treating your sweetheart terribly until she has no choice but to dump you. Another variation of this is the "cheat on your partner and let her find out" breakup. People who pull these moves often think, bizarrely, that they are sparing their partner pain by not coming out and saying "I'm leaving you," but they end up doing so much more damage. Be up-front with your partner, use your words, and don't start fucking someone new until you've settled on a custody arrangement for your dog.

If you live together, have a plan in place before you initiate the breakup. Are you going to move out, or are you asking her to leave? How soon? If you're going to continue cohabitating for a few days or weeks, where will you sleep? She'll probably have her own opinions on these questions, but knowing what you want to do at least provides a jumping-off point.

Have an exit strategy and stick to it. It's a good idea to let a friend know that you're going to break up, and have someone on call to come get you if things get too intense. This is especially important if you think there's any chance your partner will hurt you when you say you're leaving. If you feel physically or emotionally threatened or are worried that your soon-to-be-ex will try to manipulate or coerce you into staying, it's also okay to write a breakup note and be gone before she gets home.

But even if you're in no way afraid of your partner, it's good to have a plan that involves giving each other a cooling-off period. Sometimes, in the course of breaking up, your partner will try to convince you to stay with her, and sometimes she will succeed. This can be good—maybe you'll realize that this relationship could make you happy if a few things changed, and you'll agree to work through it together and come out stronger on the other side. But more often, it ends up doing nothing but drawing out the breakup. A night apart to think about what you really want, so you don't have to make the "should I stay or should I go?" decision in the heat of the moment, can be extremely clarifying. Make sure you work one into your plan.

As for how to actually say what you're thinking, just accept that there is no good way to tell someone you don't want to be together anymore. Be as honest as you can, but don't spend too much time justifying yourself. If you don't want to be together, you shouldn't be together. That's all either one of you really needs to know.

All Aboard the Dump Truck

Deciding to leave a relationship can be heartbreaking, no doubt about it, but having someone else decide to leave you is sometimes even more painful. (Usually, I feel like the worst role in the breakup is whichever one I'm currently occupying.) In your life, you will dump and be dumped in turn. Sometimes being rejected will feel like the end of the world, but it is, shockingly, possible to get through it with dignity and even a little bit of grace.

The most important thing to remember about being the one who gets left is this: If she doesn't want to be with you, you're better off without her. No matter how untrue it feels in the moment, no matter how desperately you want her back, being with someone who wishes she were somewhere else is a slow, exhausting trudge toward emotional devastation. However callous or insensitive her reason for the breakup might be, she's still doing you a favor. I'm not saying you need to send her a thank-you card; I'm just saying, don't waste your precious energy pleading with her not to go. If she wants to go, she should go. It will hurt like a motherfucker, but eventually you'll be okay. If she wants to go but stays for your sake, it will hurt like a motherfucker every day for however long it takes until one of you finally pulls the plug.

Don't try to manipulate someone into staying with you. Don't threaten to hurt yourself, turn her friends against her, steal her cat, or sleep with her ex. If you're worried that you might hurt yourself, or if you struggle or have struggled with depression, substance abuse, or other health issues and are afraid your breakup will be a trigger, seek support from your friends and loved ones, and consider looking for professional help. A girlfriend is not a doctor, and she is not responsible for your mental or physical health; her staying will not address the underlying problem or even keep it at bay for very long.

Also, don't list the kind or generous things you've done for her as reasons she owes it to you to stay in this relationship. Love can't be purchased with money, gifts, rides to the airport, or orgasms that register on the Richter scale. It has to be entered into freely and left the same way. It doesn't matter whether the pros of your relationship outweigh the cons in your mind. If she wants to leave, that's the only thing that matters.

It's always a bad idea to try to scare your partner out of leaving you. Don't say "You'll never find someone else like me." Don't say "No one else will love you like I do." It's okay if you can't find it in your heart to wish her well right now, but don't wish her ill, or at the very least don't do it out loud. It will not make her want you back. It will make her think you're a petty, vindictive jerk and that she's not only right to leave you, but that she's never going to return your blender.

Finally, don't spend too much time asking why. Sometimes the reason won't be hard to figure out (did she walk in on you in bed with your ex? Okay, there's your explanation), and sometimes she'll tell you what you did wrong, but sometimes—probably more often than not—there won't be anything big she can point to. Falling out of love tends to happen slowly, in a series of small moments. If someone's not in love with you anymore, it doesn't really matter why. Cry your heart out, but then pick it back up and start moving forward.

The Reverse U-Haul: The World's Worst Lesbian Sex Position

Breakups are never easy, but breaking up with someone you live with is much more difficult. Your eyes were so bright with hope back in the days when, carefree and foolhardy, you U-Hauled with the woman you thought you'd steal the covers from for the rest of your life. Now, older, sadder, and hopefully a little wiser, you have to pack everything up and reverse U-Haul the hell out of there.

Yes, you do have to move out. Yes, really. Yes, even if you couldn't possibly afford a place this nice on your own. Yes, even if it will upset your goldfish. Yes, even if your favorite Doc Martens are technically her Doc Martens and you're not sure you can live without them. You *cannot* continue living with your ex. Whatever sacrifices you have to make so you can have your own space in which to move on emotionally, they will be entirely worth it.

Obviously, it's great if your ex is the one to move out and you get to keep your old place, but you can't always make that happen. If she said she'd clear out but she's dragging her heels—if it's been three weeks and all she's done is put one sweatshirt in a box—it might be better for you to take the initiative, get on Craigslist, and start bubble-wrapping your plates.

If the perfect place doesn't materialize and you need to be away from your former boo sooner rather than later, there's no shame in crashing with a friend or family member for a few weeks. Ask around—see who's got a guest bedroom or an especially comfy couch and could use some help with the rent. If you choose to go this route, you should still pack up *all* your things at what is about to become your ex's place, and put whatever you can't take with you into storage or a friend's garage. You don't want to have to come back when your heart has finally begun to heal and plead with your ex to give you back your limited-edition vinyl Sleater-Kinney box set.

Even when you're in a hurry to get out of your ex's domicile, you don't necessarily want to rent the first place you see. Spend some time thinking about what you need in a new place, and what you are and are not willing to compromise about. If it has a yard big enough for your dog to run around in, can you live without a washer and dryer? If it's located such that you can walk to work, will you be able to tolerate the lack of air-conditioning? Can you deal with having roommates, or would you rather have a smaller, crappier place all to yourself? There are no wrong answers, but knowing what you're looking for will help you feel less overwhelmed as you begin to sift through your options.

At some point, you will have to do the Splitting Up Our Stuff dance with your ex. If your breakup was unusually amiable and you get along great, it might be worth the risk to go through your things together and discuss who should get custody of what, but this can be insanely stressful and push your determination to stay friends to the breaking point. Probably a better idea: Go through everything while she's out and make a "mine" and a "yours" pile, then have her check your work while you go for a walk or treat yourself to pizza. If there are things you can't agree on, unless they're cherished family heirlooms or were super expensive, it's best to just let them go; fighting over every stray earring and shot glass is going to make the process take way longer and hurt way more than it really needs to.

Any item that you bought together should generally go to the person who uses it more, with the exception of major, expensive purchases like cars. In such cases, the person who uses it more should still get to keep it, but she should reimburse the other person for her half of the cost. If you own property together, you should talk to a lawyer, because I am so far from being an expert in those matters, I can't even *imagine* what it might be like to own property. Are you a wizard?

When you've finished splitting things up as fairly as possible, get everything out in one fell swoop. If you can afford it, hire movers—I did so the last time I changed residences, and it was the best hundred bucks I have ever spent. If money is tight, as is often the case immediately after a breakup, ask your friends and family members to help you drag boxes from one place to another. It is traditional to ply them with pizza and beer in exchange for their labor, but if even that would stretch your budget too far, no one's ever mad at being served homemade food. The important thing is that you express your appreciation for their helping you with this decidedly unpleasant chore.

If you kept any sentimental trinkets—pictures of you two together, souvenirs from your last joint vacation, and so forth—don't unpack them when you get to your new place. In fact, write "Do not open until [*date six months in the future*]" on the box in giant Sharpie letters. Don't give yourself the opportunity to use these items as props with which to wallow in self-pity. Keep them out of sight until you've moved on enough to look back on the past with nostalgia, not agony.

Start Spreading the News

Anytime something bad happens and you have to let the people in your circle know, it feels a little like pulling off a scab over and over, except without the faint and disgusting sense of satisfaction. Still, you can't keep it to yourself forever. You need to get the word out about your breakup so that your friends and loved ones can offer their support, and so that the fine ladies in your immediate vicinity will realize you're available again.

In the immediate aftermath of the end of your relationship, you may not want to talk about it. And that's cool! Still, it's probably a good idea to call or text a couple of your closest friends (*not* the friends who will give you the most shit if you don't tell them right away, but the people you genuinely trust to be supportive and loving, and who will prevent you from drowning in a bathtub full of Cuervo). Give them the briefest possible version of what happened, and be clear about what you need, whether that's a ride to a hotel, a sad movie night, or just the reassurance that you're an awesome person and you'll find love again. Don't hold back on asking for help. You're not being unreasonable, you're not a burden, and you'll be there for them when they need it; right now, it's all about getting yourself to tomorrow.

And can I tell you a secret? People love being asked for help. They love being able to contribute in a substantial way to your well-being and happiness. If you're a serial U-Hauler who needs help moving out every other month, they might start to love it less, but in general, your friends and family members will be psyched to support you through your breakup.

You are never obligated to explain to people why you broke up or give them a blow-by-blow of your last big fight. If the details of your falling out are too personal, it's fine to say "I don't want to talk about it" or "We just grew apart." It's also okay to say "It was totally mutual," even if it wasn't. Your friends will recognize that for the face-saving lie it is, but they'll also understand what it really means, which is that you're not ready to get into the specifics yet and they should drop it until you've had some time to process.

Be aware that if your friends and family members ever had any qualms about your ex, this is when you'll get to hear all about them. There's something about the news of a breakup that triggers people's trash-talking gag reflex, and every negative thought they've ever had about your onetime sweetie will come pouring out. The intention behind this is usually good—they want to support you, remind you that she wasn't as great as your memory is romanticizing her to be, and reassure you that better things lie ahead. Still, it can be really hard to absorb their ranting while still trying to deal with your own broken heart. A simple "I don't need or want you to tear her down right now; I just need you to pour me a beer / put on some Rihanna / tell me I'm pretty" should do the job. If it doesn't, it's okay to keep your distance while your emotions and theirs settle down.

As for getting the word out beyond your inner circle, you can recruit your friends to help with that, although, frankly, you probably won't need to—gossip is to queer social networks what forest fires are to Colorado in the summer. Let one or two friends know what's up, and they won't even have to mention it to anyone; other queers will just absorb the information via osmosis, and by tomorrow it will be common knowledge. You can help this process along by mentioning it on social media (turn off your notifications if you can't handle being inundated with sympathy and intrusive questions) or sending out a few texts.

Of course, you're unlikely to be the only person making this announcement. If the breakup was your fault—if you cheated, lied, or otherwise behaved badly—you have to expect that your ex will be sharing her side of the story, and it will eventually, if not immediately, get back to people you know. Try not to get too hung up on this; you don't owe anyone an apology except the person you hurt. Other people might judge you for a little while, but they'll either get over it and move on to the next local scandal or self-select out of your life. Either way, just pretending you have no idea you're the subject of gossip can go a surprisingly long way toward dulling its impact. Keep your head high, let it roll off your back, and other comforting clichés. And if some voice mails get deleted unheard, who can say for sure that it wasn't just a random technological glitch?

Two Sides of the Story

When you're in the throes of a tumultuous breakup, there's nothing more tempting than trying to recruit others to your cause. Your ex hurt you because she's a heartless monster, and people need to know the truth so they can protect themselves from her diabolical machinations—really, you're being totally selfless.

Well, maybe. Or maybe you're giving in to the unsavory urge to create sides in a conflict where none really exist. No matter how justified you feel, it is very seldom cool to drag your friends and loved ones into the middle of your breakup or ask them to take sides. The end of a relationship is one of the many scenarios in which "if you're not with me, you're against me" *feels* true but doesn't actually apply.

Please note that I am not talking about situations where your ex abused you physically, sexually, or verbally. If you were wronged in that way, it's reasonable to expect that your friends and loved ones will support you and hold your ex accountable for her actions. You certainly do not have to stay friends with anyone who is friends with your abuser, or anyone who pressures you to "just drop it" for the sake of queer community harmony. Always put your own physical and mental safety first.

But when you're dealing with a more garden-variety breakup, resist the urge to air your ex's dirty laundry. It's okay to tell your BFF, your mom, or your therapist all about how she was emotionally unavailable and never did the dishes, but you don't need to share these details with every girl in your lesbian swing-dance class. Don't talk trash about your ex, and don't try to lure other people into talking trash about her, either. Just because you two turned out to be romantically incompatible doesn't mean she's an awful person who doesn't deserve friends.

This also applies to social spaces and gatherings. It's cool to avoid events where you know you'll run into your ex, at least for a little while, but if six months after your breakup you're still loudly saying "Is Megan going to be there? Because you *know* I can't go if Megan's going to be there," followed by a dramatic sniffle, people are going to slowly but surely stop inviting you out. You can't reasonably expect your social circle to expel someone for the crime of being your ex, or to bend over backward to make sure that you never, ever cross paths with her.

If the specter of inconveniencing and annoying all your friends isn't enough to prevent you from reciting your ex's flaws publicly, consider this: In queer social circles, once you develop a reputation for drama-mongering and dragging everyone else into your breakups, hot girls are much less likely to want to date you, lest they risk becoming another casualty of your crusade for your exes' social isolation. Plus, the more you rant about your ex, the more it looks like you're not over her, and women will swerve to avoid being struck by the emotional fallout. If, instead, you keep your mouth shut and treat your ex with distant but cordial respect, you look mature, together, and forgiving. Chicks totally dig that.

Rebounds Abound

No-strings sex might not be your thing, but it can still be healthy and smart to spend a little time casually dating when you've just gotten out of a major long-term relationship. If you're up-front with the people you date, this doesn't have to hurt anyone. It's the sexual equivalent of a palate cleanser—you need to get the taste of your last girlfriend out of your mouth (not like that!) before you're ready to commit fully to someone new.

Abstaining from dating and sex after a relationship can be good, because the solitude allows you to focus on yourself and figure out what you're really looking for, which may sound like a consolation prize for being single but in actuality is a huge, important step toward being a successful human being. If you want to take some time out of the dating scene to clear your head and reassess your priorities, that's great. However, don't make the mistake of thinking that taking a break from seeing people naked will prevent your next hookup from being a rebound—there's still a good chance it will be.

It's hard to work through whatever emotional hangover is left from your breakup when you're alone in your apartment. Sure, you can write in your journal or sweat out your feelings on the treadmill, but the first time you go on a date with someone new, even if it's a year from now, you're liable to feel those old trust issues or sexual hang-ups or communication problems bubbling up again. Relationship skills, it turns out, need to be practiced in relationships; you can't become a better girlfriend if you're living like a nun. By going on a few rebound dates, you give yourself a chance to exercise whatever muscles might be sore from your breakup.

If you don't take some time to rebound and date a few people you're not really serious about, you run the risk that you'll be celibate for a few months or years, meet someone you really, *really* like and want to continue seeing naked forever, and then, on approximately the third date, explode like a shaken-up Coke bottle full of crazy. Rebounding gives the crazy a chance to dissipate rather than build up. Plus, while you're going through your post-breakup figuring-yourself-out stage, it lets you try out different kinds of casual partners to see if someone you never would have imagined yourself with is actually a perfect match. Hippie vegan with an organic gardening blog? Death metal chick with piercings in places it would never occur to you to pierce? Republican small business owner? What the hell, give it a whirl.

The rules for rebounding are much like the rules for casual dating. Be honest with your dates, treat them kindly and respectfully, and don't get their hopes up for a future you have no intention of sharing. Let them know that you just got out of something serious and are playing the field for the time being. Have safer sex. If you need to break something off, be honest and direct about it—don't just stop returning someone's texts and assume she'll get the memo. And follow your heart. If what was supposed to be just a rebound hookup seems to be developing into a relationship with real potential, you don't have to run away from it. Sometimes lasting love grows where you don't expect it. Tell her how you're feeling and see if she feels the same way.

Keep in mind that rebound dates often go wrong in catastrophic, hilarious-in-retrospect ways. It's all the leftover relationship emotions we were talking about earlier. Don't stress about it too much—this is what you're here for. The stakes are low, so it's okay to make mistakes. Whatever weirdness is happening around you, go ahead and lean into it.

You Can't Spell "Sex" Without "Ex"

Look, we're all adults here, and we can admit that sometimes, the vagaries of the human heart being what they are, you are going to sleep with your ex. You're especially going to sleep with your ex if you're a queer girl, because your dating pool is just not that big and there's only so much you can accomplish with a Hitachi Magic Wand and a subscription to Crash Pad Series. Hooking up with your ex can actually be a viable part of the healing-and-moving-on process, but just like everything else in your romantic life, it's important to approach it thoughtfully, not just fall into her bed because you both happened to be drunk at the same Pride after-party.

If you and your ex basically get along—if your breakup was somewhere in the vicinity of mutual, and didn't involve a lot of fighting or months of crying your eyes out—then sleeping with her is just as valid a choice as any other casual hookup. However, if she ripped your heart out and the wound is still throbbing, or if the way she behaved during your breakup left you disgusted, delete her number from your phone and double down on your OkCupid profile. Don't sleep with people for whom your primary emotion is disdain. It doesn't matter how amazing she is in bed; if you don't actually like her anymore, you won't like yourself much after sleeping with her.

Also, don't bone an ex who has started dating someone else. I have seen people put themselves through truly awe-inspiring rhetorical contortions to justify this behavior and prove that it's not really cheating, but here's the thing: It is. You don't have eternal dibs just because you got there first. If she has a new girlfriend and her new girlfriend thinks they're monogamous, stay away. This is equally true if her new girlfriend is the one she left you for. It's not revenge, it's not justice; it's just sleazy. On the off chance that karma and/or the afterlife are real, and for the sake of your self-respect, don't help people cheat on their partners.

It's also not a good idea to have ex sex if either of you is hoping to get back together. If she wants you back and you're moving on, seeing you naked is going to conjure up all those old feelings, and she's going to have a hard time resolving them. The same is true if you're still in love and she's not. Even if you're both thinking about getting back together (relapses happen and are nothing to be ashamed of), it's got to happen through communication, compromise, and all those other things queer chicks are so good at. Your path back to true love does not begin with a two a.m. booty call.

But if both of you are happier apart than you were together, neither of you is dating anyone serious, and you can agree that it's all in good fun, there's no reason you and your ex can't keep each other's beds warm until the next big thing comes along.

Why Can't We Be Friends?

Exchanging orgasms with your former sweetie is one thing, but can you ever actually be friends with your ex? It's more likely than you might think—especially among queer women. For whatever reason, the social categories that mainstream culture likes to keep clearly separated tend to blur and spill into each other when it comes to gay and bi women. Friend, girlfriend, person I'm sleeping with, ex—all of those categories contain some overlap (if yours don't yet, give it two years). In fact, Ask A Queer Chick has gotten so many questions about former lovers who are now BFFs that I've started referring to them en masse as the Dreaded Ex-Turned-Bestie (dreaded mostly by the now-besties' new girlfriends).

Of course, depending on how acrimonious the breakup was, remaining friends with your ex is not always a desirable or viable option. And even if things didn't end in screaming and plate-throwing and setting fire to photo albums, it's always okay to decide that your ex needs to stay in your past. But if, once the dust settles, you realize that she's still the only person you want to play tennis or watch *Faking It* with, you might find that your breakup was the beginning of a beautiful friendship.

Just like with ex sex, the Dreaded Ex-Turned-Bestie relationship is only a good idea if neither of you has lingering romantic feelings for the other. Getting together for brunch is not laying the foundation for a sexy reunion—unless it is, which is also fine, but if you're not on the same page, it can lead to more heartbreak and a rerun of your initial split. If you're hanging out with the person you used to bang, think very carefully about why. Is it just because she's the only person you know who's as nerdy about baseball statistics as you are? Or are you hoping that the more time you spend having fun together, the more she'll realize what a horrible mistake she made, and she'll want to take you back? If it's the latter, do yourself a favor and extract yourself before things get embarrassing. Otherwise, you'll wake up single five years from now and realize that you've never been emotionally invested in any of your subsequent relationships because you're still saving your heart for her. Likewise, if you know she's still in love with you but you're just not feeling it, you may have to take the initiative and do what she can't—set her free to find someone who will love her back.

Even if you and your ex have settled into a perfect and mutually satisfying platonic thing, some people will assume that you're still hanging out because you haven't fully committed to the breakup. That doesn't mean you can't be friends, obviously, and you should always feel free to ignore whatever assumptions people make about you—except, just possibly, when it comes to your new girlfriends.

New girlfriends are often profoundly intimidated by the Dreaded Ex-Turned-Bestie, and it's not hard to see why. Competing with someone who knows your boo better than you do is always scary, but if that person also has years of experience getting her off, it's easy to wonder if, as the new-comer, you'll forever be stuck in second place. Therefore, if you're tight with your ex, you'll need to work extra hard to reassure any new people you date that your BFF is not com-petition, and that you care about them both in totally differ-ent ways. You can reinforce this message by having solid boundaries between Friend Time and Sweetie Time, and never bailing on dates to chat on the phone with your ex.

And sadly, at least a handful of you will eventually leave your new girlfriend to get back together with the Dreaded Ex-Turned-Bestie-Turned-Girlfriend-Again. Of course, you should follow your heart wherever it leads you, but you should also be aware that you're reinforcing ex-related trust issues not only for your most recent girlfriend but for an en-tire generation of queer women. I hope that makes you happy.

Trial and Error

Before I get into the meat of this section, I want you to promise me that you won't read it if you're fresh off a big breakup. Okay? Can we agree that if you're less than, say, a month out from your last serious relationship, you'll stick a bookmark here, skip to page 127, and come back in another month or so? Good. See you then!

Now that it's just us not-recently traumatized chickens, let's talk about what you can learn from a breakup. I don't want the newly single reading this, because when you're in that just-been-dumped headspace, it's really easy to misinterpret "this could be an opportunity for a little self-improvement" as "you are terrible and need to change everything about yourself before you'll be able to find love." However, breakups *can* be a chance to learn and grow so that your next relationship will be more successful. It depends on what kind of relationship—and what kind of breakup—you had.

Some relationships end for reasons that are genuinely neither party's fault, but rather the result of simple incompatibility. If you're not with her anymore because she wanted to move to Spain and you didn't, neither of you made a mistake—you just weren't right for each other. On the other end of the spectrum are breakups where one person is clearly in the wrong. If your partner cheated on you, lied to you, or abused you, don't waste a lot of time trying to figure out what you did to deserve it, because the answer is "nothing." (Although, if you habitually gravitate toward cheaters, liars, and/or abusers, it might be worth talking to a therapist to see if you can work through whatever kind of unintentional self-sabotage you have going on.)

But in a lot of breakups—I'm going to guess wildly that we're talking about a majority of all breakups—mistakes are made on both sides. Probably, when you think back on it with a clear head (and not with the self-righteous rage or the despondent self-loathing that immediately follow a breakup, which is why, if you had a breakup recently, you're not reading this; you're already on to the next section), you'll see that you and your ex were both good but flawed people, and that there are ways you'd like to behave differently with your next long-term naked friend.

Learning to be a stable and healthy person in a relationship can require a lot of time and a lot of trial and error. There's no need to beat yourself up over one romance that didn't work out. Like every disappointment, failure, and wrong turn in your life, it's an opportunity to grow and become even more incredible than you already are.

Think about the things your ex said to you while you were in the process of breaking up. (If reliving that conversation brings you to tears or rage or binge-drinking, you still need to cool off some. Come back to this exercise later.) Being as honest with yourself as you can possibly stand, try to separate the things she said just to hurt you—the malicious words even the kindest and most honorable of humans occasionally say in the heat of the moment—from the things she really meant. Could you have listened more carefully? Been more willing to compromise? Taken more responsibility around the house? Communicated more clearly when you were upset, instead of sulking and waiting for her to notice?

If your ex was never very clear about why she didn't want to be together anymore, the self-assessment will be more difficult but not impossible. What did you fight about? When did you feel that you were growing apart? What conversations nag you when you're on the edge of sleep, making you wish that you could just go back and change one thing you said? Again, the point here is not to torture yourself; it's to think calmly and carefully about your relationship skills. Was there anything you should have done differently? And if so, how will you keep from making the same mistake next time?

It can be useful to write about this process in a journal, if you're that kind of lesbian, or talk about it with your therapist or BFF. Having some outside input might help you come up with an action plan to use when you're falling back into bad habits, and subvert your impulse toward the behaviors that hurt your last relationship.

But don't let self-improvement spiral out of control and leave you endlessly examining your past mistakes with a magnifying glass. Do your best to identify problems and come up with possible ways to prevent them, but don't dwell on the past forever. When you find yourself circling back to the same territory again and again, you've stopped being productive and are merely torturing yourself. If you're writing in your journal, print "THE END" and start a new page. If you're discussing it over drinks with a friend, say, "That's enough about me. How's your job going?" and offer to split some artichoke dip. Learn from the past, but don't become trapped there.

Moving Up, Moving On

Moving on after a breakup is a bizarre and mysterious process. This is because you never really notice yourself doing it; you just spend a lot of time desperately wishing you could do it, flailing around in futile attempts to accomplish it, and then all of a sudden you realize that it's already happened.

The mourning period after ending a relationship generally involves a balance of productive activity and moping. You really do need to do both. If all you do is wallow, you'll be so focused on what you've lost that there will be no chance of replacing it with anything exciting or distracting or new. Plus, the less energy you expend, the less energy you'll have, and one day you'll realize that you've been wearing the same yoga pants for a week and a half (even though you haven't done yoga since college) and everything you've eaten in that time period has had the word "Cheez" in its name. On the other hand, if you obsessively seek distractions and never sit still with your pain, your unacknowledged emotions will compress inside you until one day they explode and you find yourself full-on ugly-crying in the produce department of Trader Joe's because there's a display of lemons and yellow was her favorite color.

So incorporate a little from column A and a little from column B. A night in with a bottle of wine and a sad movie marathon, followed by an afternoon of playing Frisbee in the park. A series of poignant song lyric tweets, then a road trip to visit your sister. Balance comfortable with challenging. Try something new, something you never would have tried when you were with her: Learn to cook a dish she would have hated, get a cat she would have been allergic to, throw yourself into a craft or sport. Indulge (with moderation) in your favorite vices. Even if she didn't live with you, do a really deep clean on your apartment, and get rid of every trace of her (aside from the box of sentimental keepsakes that you're not touching for six months). Get a new haircut, a new jean jacket, a new tattoo. Do something that scares the shit out of you: Go skydiving, sing at an open mike, ask for a promotion.

If she calls, let it go to voice mail. If she emails, make a special folder and filter it in unread. You'll get back to it later, maybe. Prioritize your own needs. Turn off your phone and computer, and spend a whole weekend reading a book and taking your dog on long walks. Masturbate more than you ever thought you could, but do it without thinking about her at all. Order lots of takeout. Drink lots of water. Turn up your music really loud and dance around your room like nobody is watching, or like Beyoncé is watching and you want to impress her—whichever works for you. Marathon the absolute trashiest television.

When you feel ready to think of the world beyond your emotional and physical needs—and this may take a few weeks—it really helps to get outside yourself. Do favors for your friends and family. Make dinner for someone who has a new baby. Run errands for someone who's been sick. Buy your BFF an elaborate present, just because. Send your grandmother a long, chatty letter. Volunteer and meet new, cool, socially conscious girls.

Check in with your heartache periodically, but don't let it make all the decisions for you. Think about the person you want to be, and set yourself on the path toward her. Let your amazingness shine, not to spite your ex (okay, maybe a *little* bit to spite your ex) but because you deserve it. Dig down beneath the pain, and find the stronger, braver, more joyful version of yourself that's been in there all along. Introduce her to the world.

Chapter 6

∽

Bi Any Means Necessary:
Notes on Non-Monosexuality

While often lumped in with gay and lesbian folks, bisexuals (that is, people who are attracted to members of more than one gender) actually comprise a larger percentage of the population than monosexual (attracted to only one gender) gays and lesbians. Bi people experience their own unique issues, from relationship troubles to bi invisibility to biphobia from both their straight and queer friends. In this chapter we'll discuss some of those issues and how you can handle them, whether you're an equal-opportunity lover yourself or just want to support the bi folks in your life and community.

Two or More: Defining Our Terms

A lot of people will tell you that bisexuality means having an attraction to two genders—specifically, men and women. As a result, some people claim that identifying as bisexual reinforces the gender binary and excludes people with fluid

or non-binary genders. The problem is, this is not the definition of the word "bisexual" that *actual bisexual people* use.
Ask a bi-identified person and they will almost universally
tell you that being bisexual means being attracted to people of
more than one gender.

"But 'bi' means two!" Yes, and "gay" means happy and
"queer" means weird and "lesbian" means something from
an island in Greece. The meanings of words frequently evolve
beyond their etymologies, because languages are living and
changing things (find out more in my second book, *Ask a
Chick Who Was Two Credits Short of a Linguistics Minor*). Fur-
thermore, like most words for sexual orientations and other
LGBTQ identities, "bisexual" was coined by people who were
not part of that community, as a means of pathologizing folks
attracted to multiple genders. In more recent years, the word
has been reclaimed by actual bi folks (some of them genderqueer, gender-fluid, or otherwise outside the gender binary)
who wanted the power to explain and define their own identities. If you choose not to identify as bi because it feels un-
necessarily restrictive, that's fine, but please refrain from
telling other people what words they should and shouldn't
use to refer to their own sexuality—it's rude (and just a
teensy bit biphobic).

If you are attracted to members of more than one gender,
congratulations: Bisexuality is yours. It belongs to you, and
you get to shape its present and its future. You can, of course,
also decline to identify as bisexual because you prefer another word (options include "pansexual," "multisexual," and
"queer"), but for the purposes of this chapter, I'm going to
use "bisexual" to refer to all of us folks—including me!—who

feel tingly about ladies, dudes, and lots of other cute people besides.

There's No Such Thing as Bi Privilege

What's up, monosexual gay people? I love you all like crazy. You are smart and funny, and your shoes are great. There's nothing about your delightful selves that I would change in a million years, except, oh, just that one thing where some of you keep insisting that "bi people have it so much easier."

Look, I know what you mean. I do. You mean that bi people can date people of another gender, and pass for straight, and thus avoid experiencing discrimination. Must be nice, right? But the thing is, it's not true, and it certainly doesn't count as "bi privilege."

For one thing, someone who is attracted to people of multiple genders but feels free to pursue relationships with only one *is* experiencing discrimination. They're being driven into the closet by internal or external pressures that interpret their real desires as something shameful. This is an awful way to live. Suppressing your real identity to fit into an arbitrary ideal is painful enough, all on its own, to negate the existence of so-called bi privilege.

However, the "privilege" of living in the closet is only one of the challenges bi people face. In addition to unwanted invisibility, which leads to bisexual people being underrepresented in queer spaces and movements despite being the largest group within the LGBTQ community, bi folks also experience more negative physical and mental health outcomes than monosexual gay and lesbian people. According to the San Francisco Human Rights Commission's 2011 report "Bisexual Invisibility: Impacts and Recommendations," "[Bisexual] erasure has serious consequences on bisexuals' health, economic well-being, and funding for bi organizations and programs." The report cites multiple studies finding that bisexual people are more likely than straight or gay people to experience depression, thoughts of suicide, anxiety, and hypertension, and to engage in smoking and risky drinking. Bisexual women are also more likely to be victims of intimate-partner violence than women in other demographics. In addition, bisexual people are less likely to come out to their health care providers than monosexual gay and lesbian folks, meaning they're less likely to receive all the information they need to make safer sex choices and protect themselves from STIs. They're also less likely to have health insurance than gay people, and more likely to face financial obstacles when accessing health care.

So why exactly is being bi so hazardous to your health? It's difficult to say for sure, but some researchers speculate that bi people face much of the same marginalization as monosexual gays and lesbians, but without the mitigating influence of access to a supportive queer community. Bi erasure and bi invisibility aren't just annoying; they're doing real harm. In order to undo that harm, we need increased focus on bisexual health and more bi-specific resources, so if you're in the health care field, get on that! Otherwise, you can help the Cause by spreading awareness of these issues and trying to fight bi erasure within your own community. Remember that bi folks are not appropriating your struggle; they're in this with you. Do what you can to support them.

Coming Out . . . and Out and Out and Out

We talked about this a little in Chapter 1, but it's worth revisiting here, because revisiting the experience of coming out is something bi folks need to get good and comfortable with. Even in nominally queer-friendly spaces, the presumption of monosexuality is strong, and if you're bisexual, correcting that misconception isn't as simple as dropping your girlfriend's name into a sentence and waiting a beat for everyone to catch up. If you've historically dated guys, beginning to date girls does not cue the "oh, she must be bi" realization for most people; instead, many of them will wonder why you hid the fact that you were gay. You see this in the media all the time, too; every few months another website runs a listicle of "Twenty Celebrities You Didn't Know Were Bisexual," and it's always people who have been openly bi for years (Angelina Jolie! Alan Cumming!), but because they're in long-term relationships and not actively dating people of multiple genders, their history of identifying as bi has been routinely swept under the rug.

I went through this when I first started dating women. Although I'd used the word "bisexual" to describe myself for years, my first forays into real girl-on-girl action were met with shock and confusion by much of my social circle. "You're queer? Since *when*? Didn't you have a boyfriend for, like, a year?" Yes, since always, and what does that have to do with anything? Later, I spent several years calling myself a lesbian, because I'm in a long-term same-sex relationship and I never intend to date a dude again—what did it matter if I still think Taye Diggs must have traded his firstborn to a wizard in exchange for his preternaturally perfect face? That started to feel both dishonest and restrictive, so in the last couple of years I've been getting more and more comfortable claiming—insisting on—my bi identity.

If you're willing to defend your bisexuality often and aggressively enough, after a year or two word will get out and people won't bug you about it as much. I wish I could teach you a simpler, no-fuss way of getting people to respect your non-monosexual orientation. Sadly, the fact of the matter is that you're going to have to get used to saying, on a fairly regular basis, "Actually, I'm bi, and it's not just a phase, and I'm not straight when I date men and gay when I date women; I'm just bisexual all the time"—either that or resign yourself to being the Incredible Sexual Chameleon who picks up the orientation of whatever relationship is at hand. Neither option is great. Bi invisibility is really the worst superpower.

Dating while bisexual presents its own variation on this difficulty, because you have to decide how soon into the relationship to mention that you're bi. I am of the opinion that you should make sure to mention your orientation as early as possible, in case your date is one of those all-too-common lesbians (or less-common-but-still-troublesome straight boys) who believe an aversion to bi folks is a reasonable preference rather than a character flaw. You should disclose your bisexuality not because it's a drawback to dating you (it's not—you rock!) but so that the stealth bigots will reveal themselves, allowing you to order the most expensive thing on the menu, then sneak out the bathroom window and leave them with the check.

If someone has a problem with your orientation, it might

be painful, but you should just keep reminding yourself that it's their problem, not yours. It is never your responsibility to "win over" a monosexist date; your life is not someone else's teachable moment.

The never-ending coming-out party that is life as a bi person can get exhausting, but the best way to conserve your emotional resources and your sanity is to correct people quickly and firmly and then move on. If someone says, "As a lesbian, how do you feel about the new Sarah Waters novel?" you say, "Actually, I'm bisexual, but I don't think anything new she writes will ever replace *Tipping the Velvet* in my heart." And I'm not joking about the never-ending party: Every time you have to come out to someone, especially if it's someone you're already out to, you should throw yourself a shindig, or at least have a cupcake. You deserve a little reward for all the nonsense you put up with.

Bi Now, Gay Never

One of the most common misconceptions about bisexuality is that it's some kind of stepping-stone on the way to coming out "all the way," as gay and/or lesbian. This pernicious stereotype, sometimes referred to as "bi now, gay later," is often used to warn straight people away from dating bi folks, because they'll always "go gay" in the end. While I see the appeal of fitting the chaos and unpredictability of human life into a tidy, linear narrative, a queer person's life is not a journey from straight to gay with a rest stop at bisexuality for a cold drink and a bathroom break along the way.

The truth is, bisexuality is a legitimate and distinct queer identity in its own right. It's not halfway to gay, or Diet Gay, or part straight and part gay. It's a separate thing. It deserves the same respect and recognition as any other orientation. Sure, it's possible for someone to identify as bisexual at one point in her life and gay at another, for a whole host of reasons, but that doesn't mean that her bisexuality was a mistake, or a phase, or a lie. And in fact, the same San Francisco Human Rights Commission report I quoted previously found that women were more likely to move, over time, from identifying as gay to identifying as bisexual than the other way around—which also doesn't prove that those women were never really gay. A person's identity is what she says it is, even if later on she says it's something else. Someone deciding down the line that "gay" more accurately describes her identity doesn't negate the years during which she was proudly and happily bisexual.

Respect people and treat them as valid based on who they are and what they want today, not who you think they might be tomorrow. And remember that you are not the authority on anyone else's experience. No matter how much people remind you of your younger self, or your cousin, or your favorite character from *Lip Service*, they are their own person; they get to decide what they want to be called.

LUG Nuts

If "bi now, gay later" is one side of an offensive, disrespectful coin, the LUG (or "lesbian until graduation") stereotype is its counterpart. Heads, you lose; tails, you still lose.

A LUG, in case you're not in the know, is a college girl

who "experiments" with lesbianism during her wild and crazy undergraduate years, then settles down with her degree in hand into a life of stable heterosexuality. This only makes sense if you view girl-on-girl sex as essentially performative—something you do to say you've done it, like skydiving, rather than something you actually want to do and enjoy. Otherwise, the LUG would be an object of compassion, not scorn. If lady sex rocks your world but you quit doing it because you feel like it doesn't fit into your adult life, guess what, you're probably bisexual, and you need the support and respect of your community to make it safe for you to come out, not snarky commentary.

Are there women in the world who perform bisexuality without really feeling it, just because their boyfriends think it's hot? Probably. Are there *way more* women in the world who pretend they're making out with girls only because their boyfriends think it's hot, but actually desperately wish the boyfriend would leave so they can get to the good stuff? Almost definitely. I know several girls for whom those fumbling, vaguely porny, frat-dudes-cheering-in-the-background kisses were enlightening and formative, and who have gone on to have distinguished and prolific careers in the field of lady-kissing. (Plus, this loophole allowed me to make out with at least one extremely good-looking and very taken girl, and it would be awfully selfish of me to take that off the table for future generations of queer chicks.) If you hate on youthful sapphic experimentation, you're pretty much just saying you don't think women who have dated men have any claim to queer experiences.

It seems true—it's true in my social circle, at any rate—

that bisexual-identified women are more likely to end up with a dude than a lady in the long term. That does not mean that most bi women are straight and pretending to be bi for attention. It boils down to the fact that a bi gal's dating pool is predominantly male. Think of it this way: If 10 percent of the population has some same-sex attraction—that's on the high end of what most studies find—then upward of 90 percent of the dudes you meet in your life will be into ladies, versus only 10 percent of the women. When you filter for the biphobic attitudes an unfortunately large number of lesbians still harbor, it becomes clear that even if you're equally attracted to women and men, you're probably going to date mostly dudes.

Of course, statistics don't rule your love life, and bisexual women can certainly date primarily or only women if they feel so inclined. But dating men because it's easier to find men who are into you is nothing to be ashamed of, nor does it invalidate your bisexuality. Your membership to Bi Club is not going to be revoked because of a relationship with a man. (The first rule of Bi Club is that you can talk about Bi Club all you want, because most people won't believe it's real anyway.) When bi women date men, it doesn't mean they're turning their backs on the queer community. Let's all try to remove hurtful words and phrases like "LUG" and "former bisexual" from our vocabularies, and replace them with more positive terminology like "Hey, I made you brownies."

Bisexual and Monogamous

Okay, we've covered two of the myths that are costing bi folks dates: "I can't date bi girls because they're just closeted lesbians" and "I can't date bi girls because they're just attention-grabbing straight chicks." Both of these claims are resoundingly false, but they are nothing compared to the third installment in the Trilogy of Wrongness: "I can't date bi girls because they'll just cheat on me."

It's astonishing how deeply ingrained the Legend of Bisexual Promiscuity has become in our culture, to the point that some people consider "attracted to people of more than one gender" synonymous with "attracted to all people of every gender, and unable to refrain from acting on said attraction." This assumption is almost never applied to people of any other orientation ("You're a straight woman? That's crazy! So do you just, like, make out with every guy you see?"). When it comes to bisexuality, however, the normal rules of sexual and romantic conduct are apparently suspended, to the point where bi folks are presumed incapable of monogamy. This is tied to the equally erroneous stereotype that bi folks have double the sex drive of straight or gay people, or that because we'll sleep with more than one kind of person, we'll bang anyone who offers. All these assumptions are based not on the actual behavior of bi people, but on contempt for bisexuality as an identity.

Being attracted to more than one gender does not make a person an indiscriminate slut (although I have great admiration and respect for indiscriminate sluts, as well as rigorous prudes and anyone else with a fulfilling and consensual sex life). Bi people aren't, as a general rule, into *everybody* any more than lesbians are into *all* women. Bi folks are perfectly capable of abiding by social contracts, including monogamous relationships. In short, a bisexual woman is zero percent more likely to cheat on you than any other partner.

Sure, there are bisexual cheaters. There are even bisexual cheaters who blame their cheating on their bisexuality, because people who are chronically unfaithful tend to shift responsibility onto whatever or whoever happens to be nearby. But "I couldn't help cheating on you because I'm bi" is no more true than "I couldn't help cheating on you because I'm a Pisces" or "I couldn't help cheating on you because I'm under a lot of stress at work"—that is, it's not true at all. People cheat because they're jerks who haven't found a better way to deal with their boredom or unhappiness. Don't date jerks, and don't let an encounter with a bisexual jerk put you off dating other, non-jerky bisexuals in the future.

And of course, there are bisexual people who prefer polyamorous relationships—sometimes because having partners of multiple genders is important to them, sometimes just because they've got more love to give than one person can handle. Again, this is not inextricably linked to being bisexual; there are plenty of gay and straight poly folks as well. If you're all about monogamy, don't assume that a bisexual person won't be a good match for you. Likewise, if you're poly, don't assume that your bisexual date will be down with that. Basically, as usual, don't assume anything about a potential romantic partner beyond what they've explicitly stated. Instead, treat bisexual folks as complex, multifaceted, unpredictable human beings, and be willing to communicate to find the relationship model that works best for you both.

Queer Girls with Boyfriends

There was about a year in the history of Ask A Queer Chick when every third letter I got was from a girl who was happily boyfriended up but had just become aware of her bisexuality. "What do I do?" these letters, which I still sometimes get, invariably pleaded. "I can't leave my boyfriend, but I can't go my whole life without sleeping with a girl!"

If you're in this situation, here's some bad news to start us off: You cannot be in a monogamous relationship with a man and also have sex with women. The only way to do that is to cheat on your partner, and A Queer Chick does not endorse cheating under any circumstances. Stepping out on someone you love doesn't just poison your relationship; it poisons you, and makes you trust yourself less and like yourself less than you did before. I want you to be happy, and cheating is a path that leads away from happiness, so get off that path and back on the one that leads to Emotional Fulfillment Town, or at least Short-Term Enjoyment Without Major Repercussions Avenue.

There are three basic ways you can resolve this dilemma: (1) you can ask your boyfriend to renegotiate the terms of your relationship such that banging chicks is kosher, (2) you can leave your boyfriend and hook up with ladies, or (3) you can stay with your man and shelve your sapphic inclinations, at least temporarily.

If you want to have your cake and eat pussy, too, you'll need to approach it delicately with your dude. It's probably better not to approach it as an ultimatum—"let me bone girls, or get your toothbrush off my sink"—because that will make him feel defensive and not inclined to compromise. Be clear about what you're asking for before you begin the conversation. Do you want occasional one-night stands? A long-term romantic lady partner to match your dude? Are you okay with him having other partners, too? Whatever you suggest, try not to present it as an indictment of him as a boyfriend or person. You want to sleep with women because you think it will bring you joy, not because he's failing to satisfy you in bed. (If he is failing to satisfy you in bed, that's a separate issue to be discussed at another time.)

While you're having this conversation, please refrain from falling back on the untrue and unconvincing argument that sex with another woman doesn't count as cheating because it's "not *really* sex." Do not use homophobia and the erasure of girl-on-girl relationships to win yourself a hall pass. Lesbian sex is real sex, and that's why you want to have it. Similarly, be wary of any arrangement wherein you can get it on with girls, but only in your boyfriend's presence. Even if it's fun in the short term, guys who suggest this kind of arrangement often think of bisexuality as a performance for their benefit rather than an autonomous sexual orientation, and you don't want to perpetuate their misconceptions. Plus, it's going to be way easier to find a girl who wants to bone you than to find a girl who wants to bone you in front of your boyfriend; exhibitionists are not nearly as common as lesbians.

It's important to remember that even if you do everything perfectly and present your case with dazzling eloquence, your gentleman caller might not go for it. Some people just aren't comfortable with nonmonogamy. If that's the case—or if you yourself are not interested in opening up your relationship— you'll be down to two options: Break up with your boyfriend, or learn to live without ladies.

Breaking up is seldom an easy decision, but if your heart says that it's what you have to do, trust yourself. It's okay to leave a relationship that isn't giving you everything you need, even if your needs aren't what other people expect them to be. Just do me a favor and leave as soon as you know you need to—don't shop around and wait until you've got your new girlfriend lined up before you write your Dear John letter. That's not fair to your soon-to-be-ex, who, after all, is not to blame for his failure to be a woman.

But if the thought of living without your dude is too much to bear, you might have to live without ladies instead. And as unappealing as I personally find the prospect, it is actually possible to live a long and happy life without ever getting it on girl-on-girl style. Long-term monogamous relationships always involve some level of compromise and even sacrifice. Straight women give up the other men they might have hooked up with; lesbians give up their dream of marrying Portia de Rossi. If the other person is worth it to you, those sacrifices aren't necessarily easy, but they feel right and you're happy to make them. There's no wrong answer here— you simply have to find the approach that makes you happiest, and go after it with everything you've got.

If you're a bisexual girl with a boyfriend, you may also

encounter resistance when you try to participate in your local queer community. (Maybe you won't! I hope you won't. Some queer spaces are getting better about this, but others are dragging their feet.) Don't let anyone make you question your right to call yourself queer. Queerness is not granted or taken away by the person you're sleeping with; it's part of who you are. If someone gives you a hard time, you can choose to take advantage of the teachable moment and start an enlightening conversation about bi invisibility, or you can simply explain that you're queer because you say you're queer and they can kick rocks—it's entirely up to you. Don't be dissuaded by the words or actions of a few biphobic miscreants. Queer community is *your* community, and you belong there as much as anyone else.

The Love Triangle

About one out of every ten people to whom you come out as bisexual will respond, with no apparent hesitation, by propositioning you for a threesome. This stems from two things: the assumption that all bisexual folks have an insatiable appetite for as much sex with as many people as possible, and chronic, intractable idiocy. Feel free to curse out and cut off contact with anyone who makes unwanted, inappropriate sexual advances. If you're in a generous mood, you can always point out that wanting to bone men and women is not necessarily the same thing as wanting to bone men and women *at the same time,* thereby contributing to their moral and intellectual education before you throw them out the window.

Harassment aside, however, some people, bi folks among

them, do enjoy the occasional foray into group sex, and if you're a bi woman who wants to occasionally hook up with a couple, you'll have no shortage of options to choose from. Threesomes can also be a way to bring some variety into a long-term relationship, especially if you're a bi chick who wants lasting love but isn't ready to give up all but one flavor in the great ice-cream shop of gender. Of course, monosexual queer chicks can have threesomes, too! And non-monosexual folks can have threesomes where all the participants are of the same gender. The possibilities are nearly endless.

Group sex can be fun and hot, but it can also present unexpected emotional hurdles. First and foremost, you should never use group sex as a way to get close to someone you're crushing on who's already taken. It might seem like a quick fix—they get to keep their relationship, you get to see them naked, problem solved—but in fact, sleeping with someone whose feelings for you aren't as strong as yours almost always leads to heartache. And if you're hoping to sex her up so good that she leaves her boyfriend for you, you will only end up disappointed and resentful, which is not what anyone wants to get out of a sexual encounter.

If you're planning a threesome, it's not a good idea to just put on some music, drink some tequila, and let nature take its course. Things will go better if you and your coconspirators have some discussion first about what you're all hoping to get out of this encounter and what you want to avoid. Will this be a one-night stand, or are you open to the possibility of a do-over? If two of the people involved are a couple, are there sex acts they aren't comfortable sharing with anyone but each other? What kind of safer sex practices will you be using? (Remember that if you're doing anything that requires a condom or glove, you'll need to use a new condom or glove each time you switch partners.) Having this conversation ahead of time can save you a lot of awkwardness while you're doing the deed, and perhaps increase the possibility that you'll get to sleep with these two people again.

But whatever conclusions your negotiations lead to, don't fall into the trap of deciding that "no one will be jealous." Jealousy and insecurity come up in almost any sexual relationship, and are exponentially more likely to arise when more than two people are involved. You can't prevent it; just be willing to discuss these feelings when they appear and work through them together.

Everyone Gets a Gold Star

If you're not bisexual, or you haven't spent much time thinking about the problem of bi erasure within the queer community, you might not understand why I break out in hives every time someone uses the phrase "gold star lesbian." Let's talk about it so that you can join me in my never-ending crusade to wipe that Ellen-forsaken phrase off the face of the earth.

When you refer to a lesbian who has never had sex with a man as a "gold star lesbian," you are not just implying but stating outright that people who have had different-gender sexual encounters are *worse at being gay* than people who haven't. That sucks. You're shaming people who took longer than you did to figure out their orientation, or who tried to make it work with the opposite gender because they were worried about being discriminated against, persecuted, and alienated from their families and communities. That sucks, too. There's also a good chance you're perpetuating transphobia and trans erasure in the queer community, since I've heard lots of people claim that you can be a gold star lesbian if you've slept with trans men but not if you've slept with trans women. That really, really sucks.

But also, when you talk about gold stars, you're devaluing bisexuality. You're enforcing a bizarre idea of queer purity, where having "straight" sex taints your claim on queerness forever. Once again, you're feeding the misconception that bisexuality is just some weird, vaguely unclean mixture of heterosexuality and "real" queerness. Let's be very clear: It's not. Bisexuality is a queer identity in its own right, and bi girls aren't just lesbians who keep getting lost on their way to Ladytown and ending up in Dudeville instead.

If you're a lesbian who got all her spelling words right this week, go ahead and call yourself a gold star lesbian—I'm proud of you! But otherwise, please work on erasing that phrase from your vocabulary. Everyone's identity is valid, no matter whom they've banged in the past. Lesbians do not have a greater claim on queerness than bi women. And your partner's genitals do not determine either their gender or your orientation.

If we can't put this tired old saying out of its misery in the next . . . oh, let's say five years, I say we go the opposite direction: Flood the market. Give out gold stars for everything. "You made a delicious gluten-free lasagna! You're a gold star lesbian!" "Your hair looks so good today. Total gold star." Either we all get gold stars or no one does.

The Problem with "Born This Way"

One of the prevalent theories in today's gay rights ideology, and in the field of mental health, is that LGBTQ people are "born this way"; that is, our gender identities and orientations are fixed from birth and can't be changed later in life, no matter how strong the incentive. This line of thinking runs counter to the archaic perspective that queerness is a deviant and sinful "lifestyle choice," and is frequently used to defend equal rights for queer and trans folks. Since we can't change, this line of thinking goes, what's the point of oppressing us, or pushing us into harmful and ineffective conversion therapy? Nothing straight people can do will make homosexuality or gender dysphoria go away.

These arguments also frequently include an undercurrent of "don't you think we'd choose to be different if we could?" They tend to suggest that since being LGBTQ almost invariably exposes a person to rejection, suffering, and discrimination, any sane person would choose being straight in a heartbeat if the option were on the table.

The problem here is that bisexual people everywhere *do* have a choice in which gender to date, sex up, and marry—and those choices are valid even if they're not societally sanctioned. When you say "Gay people shouldn't be persecuted because they can't help it," you're implying "It's fine to persecute bi people in same-sex relationships, because they *can* help it." I hear all the time from bi people who came out to their families and were under immediate pressure to date and marry someone of the opposite gender, because "your life will be so much easier" and "at least you have the option!" This is where "born this way" politics stop being helpful and start holding us back.

Defending being gay on the grounds that it's not a choice suggests that if it *were* a choice, it would be the wrong one. This not only creates pressure for bi folks to stay closeted and have straight-looking relationships (which, as we discussed earlier, is a form of oppression, not "privilege"); it's also *super homophobic.* People whose commitment to gay rights hinges on an inability to select a different path are actually not that committed to gay rights at all. They still see same-sex relationships as lesser. This is true even if they themselves are gay, because internalized homophobia is real as hell.

I know that the "born this way" argument has been instrumental for some LGBTQ folks in bringing their less-than-compassionate friends and relatives around on the topic of gay rights, but I don't think it's worth taking an incremental step forward only to be halted in our tracks by the fact that those people still look down on our relationships. Saying "it sucks to be gay, but some of us are stuck with it" invokes pity, not compassion—and certainly not solidarity. Plus, a modicum of advancement for monosexual gays and lesbians doesn't justify perpetuating an ideology that is actively hurtful to bi people.

It doesn't matter whether someone has known they were gay since they were in diapers, or if they just made up their mind last Tuesday, or if they date men and women and every other imaginable gender as the spirit moves them. The reason it's okay to be in a same-sex relationship is that same-sex relationships are okay, whatever the history or other interests of the parties involved. Not invoking homophobic, biphobic tropes to justify your perfectly valid adult relationship is one of the many things that, in my futuristic queer utopia, will earn you a gold star. You don't have to be "born this way" to be great the way you are.

Plenty of Fluids

Many people experience their non-monosexuality as fairly stable—that is, they might be attracted to someone of any gender at any given moment, as long as that person meets their personal standards for attractiveness, politics, giving good back rubs, etc. But for other folks, their orientation shifts over time. They might be primarily attracted to men one day, and go for nothing but androgynous genderqueer people the next, based on the phase of the moon, what they had for breakfast, or who they most recently broke up with. These people are often referred to as "sexually fluid," and they, like everyone else who falls under the LGBTQ umbrella, are awesome.

If you're a person with a fluid sexuality, you're welcome to the Mantle of Bisexuality whenever you feel moved to put it on, but it's also okay for you to identify with whatever orientation best describes you on any given day. Like many bi people, you will probably experience a fair amount of pressure to "make up your mind." The thing is, you don't actually have to! You can leave your mind unmade for your whole life, or you can make it every morning and then unmake it every night.

It's crucial to the long-term success of the LGBTQ movement, and the health of the community, that bisexual, pansexual, sexually fluid, and otherwise non-monosexual people's identities and experiences be respected and honored. If we want strength in numbers, we've got to stop prioritizing the needs of monosexual gays and lesbians over the needs of the rest of the community. We're all here, we're all queer, and it's time to get used to each other—and start working together to take over the world.

Chapter 7

∞

I'm Not Gay, but My Sister Is:
Advice for Straight People

Most of the requests for advice I get are, not surprisingly, from queer people. But a sizable minority of them are from straight people who want to know what they can do to make life easier for the LGBTQ folks they know and love. This chapter is for you, straight people! I want to help you be as kind and supportive as possible. This is also for queer folks who want to know how they can do a better job of standing up for and with the other queer folks in their lives. Read on, and let's all be just a bit more excellent to each other.

What to Expect When You're Suspecting

Back in Chapter 2, we talked about gaydar—you know, that instinct you hone over time that helps you pick up subliminal signals that someone might be queer. Well, sometimes your gaydar starts blaring, but the person it's pointing at remains stubbornly silent. What do you do when you're pretty sure a friend or loved one is LGBTQ but they're taking their sweet time letting you know?

As tempting as it might seem to pull your BFF, brother, or great-niece aside and say "Hey, I know you're gay and I'm totally fine with it," it's never the right move. For one thing, it's super intrusive. Nobody likes to realize that someone they're close to—or worse, not that close to—has been speculating about the content of their heart, undergarments, or porn folder. People's private lives are none of your business, so don't start off on the wrong foot by trying to make it your business.

If the person you're talking to is actually not queer (or trans, or whatever it is you're wondering about), they're going to feel really weird about your assumption. It could end up making them feel self-conscious or second-guess themselves, because they're trying to figure out what is sending false messages about the person they are; it could make them feel defensive and insulted, not because being gay is bad, but because being misunderstood hurts. There's nothing wrong with being a pastry chef, but if someone came up to me and said "You seem so much like a pastry chef. Are you a pastry chef? You can tell me—I'm totally pro-pastry chef," I would be severely weirded out, because *how can you be so wrong about me and my terrible baking skills?*

And the conversation isn't likely to go much more smoothly if your suspicion is correct. A nonstandard gender or orientation tends to carry some baggage, and is not something anyone wants to become public or even private knowledge before they make the specific, conscious decision to announce it. As we discussed in Chapter 1, the choice of when and how to come out is a fraught one. Don't take that away from someone just because you're eager to confirm that you were right.

There's also the possibility that the person who sets your gaydar pinging is not entirely certain of their own gender or orientation yet. Sometimes it takes a while—months, years— to go from "I don't think I'm straight" to "I know exactly what I am, and I want to tell the world." Again, you need to respect this process. Don't push someone to define something they may not yet have words for. If you put pressure on them and they say something they later regret, guess who's the jerk? Here's a hint: It's you.

And remember that none of these things is any less true if you are also queer. Being part of the club yourself does not grant you magical powers of mind reading, nor does it make it appropriate to pry into other people's business. Don't push, and don't presume. No one owes you the deepest truth of their soul just because there's a chance you both think Naya Rivera is hot. If you want to date someone and you're not sure if she's into girls, ask her out and see what she says; otherwise, what do you need to know for, anyway?

If you want someone to disclose their personal information to you, you'll need to prove they can trust you. Demonstrate that you care about them, that you enjoy spending time with them, that you have similar values. Work on making yourself a safe person to talk to; then, whenever they decide they're ready to share their inner life with someone, your name will probably be high on the list.

The Coming-Out Conversation

When someone comes out to you, your immediate reaction can have an enormous impact on your relationship, sometimes for years to come. Be ready now, so you don't blow it when it counts.

First of all, to build on the previous section, when someone reveals to you a truth they've been keeping to themselves, it is not under any circumstances acceptable to say "Well, duh." You may have guessed; you may have had fairly substantial evidence; still, *you do not know* until the person in question comes to you herself. Telling her that she needn't have bothered going through the probably exhausting process of searching her soul, naming her truth, and deciding you were someone she could trust with it, because you've totally known ever since she got that haircut? It's not supportive and it's not going to make her think of you as a trusted friend.

So don't respond with "ho-hum," but don't go too far in the other direction, either. Don't lose your shit. And above all, don't get angry. Even if the person you're talking to has been actively hiding their orientation or gender, even if you're offended that it took this long to confide in you, do whatever you can to tamp down your initial reaction and respond in a way that's appreciative and respectful of the revelation they've just shared. "Thank you for telling me" is always a good place to start, because being honored with someone's deepest secret is a huge compliment. It's okay to ask "Who else knows?" so that you don't accidentally out somebody, but don't ask if all you want to know is who found out before you so that you can resent them accordingly. Being a trusted confidante is not about winning a competition.

Don't respond to someone's disclosure by peppering them with questions about their personal business. Most especially, don't ask "Are you sure?" People are generally pretty sure about their orientation by the time they work up the nerve to come out (although if they're not 100 percent certain, that's okay, too). Trust me: No one has ever responded to "Are you sure?" with "You know what, now that you mention it, I think my being gay was all a big misunderstanding. Oh well, back to heteronormativity!"

Other things not to ask about include the specific details of someone's sex life, "But how will you have kids?" and "Is this because you didn't have a strong father figure?" Also, please don't ever ask trans people about their bodies, whether they're on or plan to start hormones, etc. If they want you to know, they will tell you. Generally speaking, it's better to ask an open-ended question like "Is there anything else I need to know so that I can behave respectfully about this?" That way, the recipient of your curiosity knows you're interested in their life and want to hear whatever they're comfortable telling you, but they won't feel like you're prying.

When someone comes out to you, it's your job to be supportive and, if they seem at all concerned about how you'll receive the news, to reassure them that you love them as much as ever and your relationship has not changed. This is not, however, your chance to deliver a soliloquy on the topic of "How I Totally Love the Gays." You don't need to list all the LGBTQ people you know and how cool you are with them. This is not about you. It's about your loved one and what they need. So ask them what they need—don't assume you already know.

If someone specifically asks you to help get the word out regarding their identity or orientation, it's fine to do so. Otherwise, assume they want you to keep it to yourself. Many people have very strong feelings about who finds out what, and in what specific words, and in what order. Do not take that away from them, or you will find yourself blacklisted not only by the gays but by the Sisterhood of Control Freaks of America. Those chicks are no joke—they will break into your house and rearrange your spice rack so that you can *never find the smoked paprika again.*

More than anything else, it's crucial that you keep your loved one's coming out in perspective. This is a big moment for them, but in the context of your entire relationship, it's not that big a deal. They're the same person they've always been, even if some things have changed. Tell them you know that, and follow their cue for what to do next.

Oh, and if you can afford it, buy them a beer (or some ice cream, if they don't drink). They've probably been steeling themselves for this conversation for days or weeks. Now that it's over, they deserve to blow off a little steam.

Be Resourceful

One of the most important parts of being a supportive LGBTQ-friendly straight person is finding your own resources. Don't expect your gay friend, trans niece, or genderqueer coworker to do all the work of bringing you up to speed on queer issues—they're human beings, not an Encyclopedia Lesbionica.

Buy some books by queer folks, or check them out at the library. (This one is a good start! Thanks!) Ask your LGBTQ loved ones to recommend some writers they like, but don't stop there; if they point you toward a book, peruse its endnotes to get ideas for what to read next. Familiarize yourself with the basic history of gay rights in the United States, pre- and post-Stonewall, as well as current issues (which are not limited to marriage equality). In addition to books, read blogs, Twitter feeds, and websites that specialize in LGBTQ issues. I like Autostraddle, AfterEllen, the EDGE Media Network (for whom I used to write), and Laverne Cox on Twitter. Google anything you're curious about. (You should probably use a safe search.) Look up unfamiliar words. Pay attention to what the queer and trans people you love are saying—not just in one heavy-duty study montage, but every day of your life.

If someone tells you that you've said or done something offensive, educate yourself on why they might feel that way. Don't expect them to do your homework for you. And don't get defensive or tell them they're wrong to be upset—people can be hurt by something that doesn't seem like a big deal to you, because you don't have to face it every day. Also, don't wait until your foot is so stuck in your mouth you're choking on toe rings to do some research and figure out how to be a supportive ally. Be proactive in learning what's likely to annoy or offend people, and then—this is the really important part—*don't do those things*.

If you're struggling to come to terms with the identity or

orientation of someone you care about, don't make it their responsibility to guide you into the warm light of acceptance. Knowing that you're judging them is probably painful, and more likely than not, they don't really feel like talking you through it. Instead, find a support group like PFLAG in your area, where you can discuss your feelings with people who have been in similar situations, and avoid hurting your loved one in the process.

Keep in mind that no matter how much Leslie Feinberg you read, how many people you talk to, or how many queer Tumblrs you follow, you are still not an authority on the LGBTQ experience. If the blog you're reading tells you that gay women love acoustic rock but your lesbian stepsister only listens to Slayer, she's not doing a bad job of being gay. It's wonderful to be an autodidact, but nothing you read will ever replace respecting the lived experience of your friends and family members. They, not you, are the experts on their own lives.

Learn the Lingo

As you're beginning your journey of self-education, acquiring the necessary vocabulary to converse respectfully with your queer friends should be among your highest priorities. The preferred terms evolve from generation to generation, so especially if you're a premillennial, it's a good idea to brush up on your queer terminology (queerminology? No, probably not).

The way we use language is so, so important. Don't brush it off as mere political correctness or nitpicking. Even if you see two words as synonyms, there's a good chance that to someone in the know, they carry very different, nuanced connotations that make one preferable to the other. Have you ever known a woman named Elizabeth who didn't have a strong, bordering on violent opinion on whether she was a Liz or a Beth? Shades of meaning that seem insignificant to you might be the difference between being perceived as a supportive friend or an offensive douchebag, so bone up on this rich and useful dialect. Here's a quick overview.

"Gay" means a person who is only or primarily attracted to their own gender. "Lesbian" means a woman who is only or primarily attracted to other women. "Bisexual" describes a person who is attracted to their own as well as other genders—not necessarily just men and women, and not necessarily equally attracted to every gender. "Lesbian" can be an adjective or a noun, but "bisexual" and "gay" are just descriptors—you are not ever "hanging out with some gays." No one describes themselves as "homosexual." Some people do use "mo" as a slang term for a gay person, but if you're straight you should steer clear of that one. "Queer" can describe pretty much anyone who's not straight, including gay, lesbian, and bi folks as well as people who are asexual or aromantic, but not everyone who's not straight describes themselves as queer.

"Trans" refers to a person who identifies as a gender other than the one they were assigned at birth. It's generally not cool to say that a trans person was "born a boy" or "born a girl," since many trans folks feel that they were born the gender they now identify as—it's just the designation that was wrong. Likewise, "male-bodied" and "female-bodied" aren't great descriptors, because a female body is any body that has a female person inside it, regardless of genital configuration. Thus, the preferred nomenclature is "designated male/female at birth," or "DMAB" and "DFAB" for short. "Cis" means a person who identifies with their birth-designated gender—in other words, a DFAB cis woman or a DMAB cis man.

Though the above should serve as an acceptable guide for general-interest conversations, it's important to remember that individual people will have individual preferences regarding how you refer to them. When in doubt, defer to the chosen terminology of the person you're speaking to or about. This won't always match up precisely with the widespread usage—for instance, most trans people these days find the word "transsexual" distasteful and prefer "transgender," but some folks still like "transsexual" better. Thus, you should use "transgender" when referring to the general trans population, but "transsexual" for specific people who identify with that word. In much the same way, while most of the nonstraight community has adopted "queer" as a catchall descriptor, some older gay, lesbian, and bisexual folks still experience it as a slur and are offended by it. Be sensitive to personal tastes, and don't describe people using words they dislike or find insulting. If you're not sure, pay attention to the words they use and let that be your template.

There is, however, an exception to the above rule. If you're not a member of a marginalized community, it is never cool to use a slur to describe that community, even if the person you're talking to does it first. Gay and bisexual women can use the word "dyke"—I do all the time; it has a very satisfying mouthfeel—but straight people cannot. I know it's unfair, but I can think of a few unfair advantages to being straight, too, so just let us have this one, okay?

Likewise, even if you are an LGBTQ person, you cannot reclaim slurs that don't apply to you. Gay men shouldn't say "dyke." Gay women shouldn't use gay-male-specific slurs (you know the one I mean). Cis queers shouldn't use trans-specific slurs (you know that one, too). And people who don't experience a specific form of oppression definitely shouldn't chastise people who do for getting offended by slurs or other microaggressions. The words we use both affect and reflect how we see the world. They matter. Be thoughtful about how you use them.

Meeting the Partner

It's one thing to adjust, on an intellectual level, to the information that someone you love has a different orientation than you assumed. For some straight folks, though, adjusting to the visceral reality—in the form of the person your loved one is dating, banging, marrying, or "it's complicated"ing—is a much bigger challenge. However, accepting someone's sweetie gracefully is crucial to demonstrating that you accept their life and identity, and failing to do so can hurt your relationship in ways that last, so you need to be prepared to clear that hurdle.

This is a basic golden-rule situation: Think about how you'd like your significant other's family and friends to treat you, and treat your loved one's significant other the same way. Remember their name, remember their preferred pronoun, and include them in conversations and activities. Don't talk over them, or about them as though they aren't in the room.

If you're introducing your loved one's partner to somebody new, don't stumble over their name or pronoun or otherwise make it clear that you're uncomfortable with their identity or existence. As discussed above, defer to the preferred terminology of the couple: If Shannon introduced Claire as "my partner," don't say "This is Shannon's girlfriend." And especially don't refer to someone's same-gender partner as their "friend" or "roommate." There's no more efficient way of communicating that you're not on board with the relationship, and you run a serious risk of alienating both your loved one and their sugar bear. Also, it's never your job to out anybody, so if you know something about your loved one's partner (he's bisexual, she's trans, they're polyamorous, or whatever) that they might not want to be public knowledge, err on the side of keeping it to yourself.

If your loved one came out to you by bringing their partner home for Christmas, they've committed a minor faux pas, but it's your job not to compound it by overreacting. Don't freak out. Take deep breaths, make a cup of tea, go to your happy place, pour a Jesus-load of whiskey into that tea—whatever it takes to calm yourself down so that you don't attack your loved one or their partner. A bad reaction to someone coming out is harmful enough; a bad reaction that embarrasses them in front of the person they're boning is way worse, and will take longer to work through.

No matter how hard it is to come to terms with your loved one's LGBTQ identity, your struggle is not their partner's fault, so don't take it out on them and don't expect them to hold your hand through it. Trying to come between two people who are dating will not make either of them one single iota less gay, but it might make them less excited to invite you over for board-game night. If you can't be cool with your friend or family member when their partner is around, just keep your distance. Sometimes you have to hash some things out, but it's never okay to drag someone's date into the middle of your tears-and-recriminations party. If you can't find anything nice to say, stay home.

Treat your loved one's same-gender partner the same way you would treat an opposite-gender one, which means, among other things, don't be one of those people who cringes whenever two women hold hands. If it's a level of PDA that would be appropriate for a straight couple, it's fine for a queer couple, too. (If you're someone who is bothered by any amount of PDA from anyone, that's different, but also, loosen up a little, Mom.) If you treat your bisexual sister's dude partners way better than you treat her lady partners, she will notice, and she will start giving you subtly terrible Christmas presents as a means of psychological warfare (beautifully framed photographs where your hair is doing that weird thing, recordings of bands you hate covering songs you love, etc.).

And don't be the person who tries to sow discord in a relationship in the hope that it will end and your friend or family member will come crawling back to straightness. This has approximately a zero percent long-term success rate, and it's also irredeemably evil. Just stay out of it.

In fact, even if you hate someone's partner for reasons having nothing to do with gender or orientation, it's still better to stay out of it, unless you think your loved one might be in physical or psychological danger. If your problem with her girlfriend is that she's never held the same job for more than three months or she doesn't tip the waitstaff, your only real option is to keep your mouth shut until their almost-inevitable breakup, and then swoop in with consolations and introductions to more suitable queers. In the worst-case scenario— they're getting married; Deadbeat Girlfriend is now Deadbeat Wife and Deadbeat Mother to Your Grandchildren—smile a lot, say "I'm so glad you're happy!" and get someone else to give the toast at their wedding.

Look, There's No Easy Way to Say This— Just . . . Don't Be a Dick

I can help you avoid some of the potential pitfalls of being a straight person interacting with LGBTQ people, but I cannot predict every situation you might face. You'll need to build up a skill set of tolerance and kindness that will allow you to weather every unforeseen circumstance with some shred of grace, or at least without pissing off everyone around you. The most important skill you can possess is the simple ability to not be a dick.

"Not being a dick" means working hard, in your deepest and most solitary heart, to see LGBTQ people as your equals and compatriots. It means searching out the part of you that thinks being gay is less valid than being straight, and stomping it like you would a bug. It means reminding yourself, over and over, as often as needed, that you are not superior to

LGBTQ people, and that they deserve love and understanding and resources and great sex every bit as much as you do.

If you do this work externally but not internally, it will only be a costume that you wear. If you know that your niece Fiona is a trans girl but in the darkest corners of your mind you still think of her as your nephew Josh, you will one day call Fiona by the wrong name and offend her. If you would never use homophobic slurs in public, but you whisper them to yourself when someone cuts you off in traffic, you will eventually let one slip in front of your gay college roommate.

Once you've made such an error, you can't try to wave it away by insisting you're "not really like that" or "it was a onetime thing." You don't have to dwell on it with the offended party—apologize sincerely, but then let it go—but you should take a hard look at yourself and how you can improve. If you used a slur or misgendered someone, you're the kind of person who uses slurs or misgenders people. The correct response is to work on fixing yourself, not insist that others excuse your transgressions because it was only that one time. If you punch someone in the face, you don't get to be like, "But what about all those times I *didn't* punch you in the face?" If you hit someone, you're violent. If you use homophobic slurs, you're homophobic. Whether or not it was a onetime thing, it's a reflection on your character, and if you're embarrassed by it, you need to work on getting some better character.

Whenever you notice a homophobic (or transphobic, or biphobic) thought entering your mind, consciously replace it with a better one. Think of the part of your brain that generates those ideas as your terrible, annoying, offensive younger sibling that you need to teach to behave in polite company. It will act up for a lot longer than you'd probably like, but you just need to keep reminding it to be its best self. When it says "Ugh, gay people are fine, but do they have to kiss in public?" tell it—out loud, if you're where no one else can hear you— "They're happy and they're not hurting anybody, so why do you care?" When it says "If she's bi, she can just decide to date men," tell it, "If she likes dating women, she should be able to, because she's an adult and her choices are valid." Repeat this as often as necessary. Note that this is not about self-flagellation; it's about becoming a better person. If you fall short of your ideals, don't punish yourself or try to justify it—just try harder next time.

Saying "don't punish yourself" does not, however, mean that you don't have to make amends if you hurt someone. Using homophobic language, reacting badly when someone comes out to you, denigrating someone's partner, using the wrong name or pronoun—these are all things that show disrespect for a person's identity and choices, and other people may very well be angry at you when you disrespect them. Their anger is valid; you don't get to decide whether someone's feelings should be hurt. If that person is important to you, apologize, make it clear you know what you're apologizing for (don't say "I'm sorry if you were offended," which is a great way to advertise that you're a passive-aggressive sack of assholes but not fantastic for mending relationships), and explain how you plan to heal the damage you've done and/or avoid screwing up in the same way again. Even if your offense is a long time past—either because it took you a long time to realize you acted like a jerk, or because you were too embarrassed to address it right after it happened—cowgirl up and apologize, because I guarantee you the object of your mistake has not forgotten it.

It's always possible, of course, that a person you've harmed or offended in the past will choose not to forgive you, even if you try in good faith to make it up to them and grow as a person. That is their prerogative. No one ever owes another person their forgiveness, their friendship, or their esteem. Do not sulk or throw tantrums if your attempt to make amends is not accepted. Regret what you've lost, but move forward with the resolution not to commit the same errors again. Tomorrow is another chance to be less of a dick.

Get Up, Stand Up

As a straight person, you have more power, privilege, and visibility in the world than your LGBTQ friends and loved ones. You didn't ask for it, but it's there, and to paraphrase a saying that I'm pretty sure is under copyright, with great ability to do things comes great obligation to do things for other people. In other words, you should use your unearned advantage as a straight person to improve the world for queer folks.

Bigoted people tend to assume that everyone else is bigoted, too—that it's common to think the way they do, but they're the only ones with the conviction to say it out loud. They're wrong, of course, but every time you allow their assumptions to go uncontested, their confidence grows. If a white person makes a racist joke among other white people and no one says "Dude, that's a terrible thing to say," he figures they're fine with it, and he's that much more likely to do the same thing again. The same goes for gay jokes. Your homophobic cousin might not throw around the word "gay" as a pejorative in front of me, so I won't have the chance to yell at him for it, but when he does it in front of you, make sure to let him know it's unacceptable.

It's probably going to feel awkward the first few—or the first few thousand—times you say "Hey, not cool" when someone makes a joke at LGBTQ people's expense. You may feel like it shuts down conversations, or makes people uncomfortable being around you, or even makes people like you less. But guess what? That's pretty much what being queer is like all the time. You'll get used to it.

Obviously, it's also great to push back against homophobic and transphobic behavior when LGBTQ people are present, because then we won't have to feel alone and potentially unsafe in standing up for ourselves. Offering backup when someone is under fire is almost always appreciated. But what you do when your queer friends aren't around is arguably more important. Lots of bigots know better than to blast their archaic ideas in front of "the gays," but far fewer understand that their point of view is repellent to *all* right-thinking people. That's the message we need your help in spreading.

You don't have to wait for an LGBTQ person to say "That was fucked up" before you speak or post a Facebook comment. You can be the person who points out that if someone's fun depends on denigrating or caricaturing queer people, it's not fun worth having. There will probably be some pushback of the "Come on, it was just a joke" variety, but if you really want to support and show up for LGBTQ people, you'll stand your ground. This kind of humor, where our existence is the punch line, isn't actually funny. Eventually, people will either get their act together, or they'll dismiss you as a humorless buzzkill, which is fine, because then you don't have to hang out with homophobes anymore.

Sometimes the person with the appalling opinions on LGBTQ people is someone you just don't feel comfortable cutting out of your life—queer folks go through this, too, and it's a tough line to walk. The best thing you can do in that situation is assert your boundaries and redirect the conversation. In practice, this looks like "I disagree, but I don't think there's anything to be gained by discussing this further. Shall we order appetizers?" or "You know I don't like it when you talk about my friends that way. Let's take the kids to the park instead." You don't necessarily have to cut ties with anyone just because they're stuck in a Stone Age concept of human relationships, but the continuous reminder that their opinions are not shared and not welcome may be the nudge that eventually pushes them to reconsider—and if not, at least you'll be able to sleep at night knowing you didn't condone homophobia today.

The *A* Is Not for "Ally"

As important as the support of straight people is to LGBTQ folks' increasing civil rights, visibility, and liberation, it's also crucial that our allies know when to take a backseat. This movement is not about you, and when straight people try to be the center of attention it's distracting and counterproductive.

Sometimes you'll see "LGBTQ" expanded to "LGBTQIA." The *I* stands for "intersex" (people with physical characteristics of more than one sex); the *A* stands for "asexual" (people who don't experience sexual attraction). Both these groups of people experience oppression that is distinct from, but in some ways related to, the oppression that gay, bi, and trans people face. Including them in the acronym and the community allows us to pool our resources, support each other, exchange hair-care tips, etc. Our struggles aren't always identical, but they're similar enough to create camaraderie and the intra-community relationships that help us all to survive.

The *A* in LGBTQIA does not stand for "allies." Allies are not members of the LGBTQIA community because they do not face the oppression that defines that community. Some allies do catch flak for standing up to homophobia and bigotry, but it's always optional—they can choose to avoid it through silence, which is not a path available to queer folks.

What this means is that, as valuable as your support and understanding are, it's vital that you don't take up too much space in the LGBTQIA movement. It's not your job to speak on behalf of—or over—the people you want to help. You don't get to define the priorities or the goals of LGBTQ people, no matter how good your intentions are. Your approach should be to defer to the leadership of queer and trans people, then back them in whatever ways are available to you.

Being an ally does not give you the right to critique LGBTQ people's reactions to homophobia, transphobia, and discrimination. No amount of "Come on, I'm on your side!"

makes it okay for you to tell someone they shouldn't be so offended by that gay joke. The people who are hurt by oppression get to decide how hurt they are, and when, and why. Your support for their cause is no substitute for lived experience, and you have no idea how many times a person might have heard that seemingly innocuous comment before she snapped. There's no way for you to understand how homophobic microaggressions feel in the context of a lifetime of discrimination, so even if you think someone is overreacting, keep that opinion to yourself.

Being an ally also does not mean you're off the hook if you do something offensive. I don't care how many pro-gay-marriage rallies you've attended; if you tell me that trans women shouldn't be allowed in the women's restroom, we're in a fight. It's fantastic if you do good things, but they don't cancel out the bad things you do. Apologize like a grown-up, realize that mistakes are inevitable, and resolve to deal with them productively. While you're at it, be grateful for the people who care about you enough to point them out. If I think you're just an intractable asshole, I'm not going to ask you to stop using "queer" as a noun—I'm going to avoid you altogether. When people get mad at you or ask you to change your behavior, it means they believe you have the potential to do better. Cherish their faith in you. Buy them dinner.

Finally, remember that real support is not performance art. You don't do it to impress people. You don't do it to show off. You do it because it's the right thing to do, and you don't demand pats on the back for it.

One day I was walking hand-in-hand with my partner, and a dude slowed down to yell "I support you!" from the window of his car. That was all about him, not us. It didn't make our lives better or easier in any way. In fact, it made us feel decidedly uncomfortable and more than a little objectified. We would have had a better day if he'd kept his window up, gone home, and donated to Lambda Legal. His shouting was intended to show people what a good straight person he was, but it didn't actually contribute anything to the Cause.

Don't be that guy. Don't bring me support like a puppy carrying a stick, wanting praise and pats on the head. Being a real alliance often feels thankless, but if your goal in life is to be showered with praise, don't make that LGBTQ folks' problem—take it up with your therapist. You're an extra in this production. If you feel that our liberation is more important than your ego, go ahead and pick up your spear.

Chapter 8

∾

Haters Gonna Hate:
Dealing with Discrimination

There are so many wonderful things about being a member of the LGBTQ community—our friendships, our culture of liberation and resistance, our hairstyles, *Carmilla*. But as important as it is to celebrate everything that's great about queer life, there's no denying that being LGBTQ can also be hard, exhausting, and scary. At some point in your journey, you will undoubtedly encounter discrimination or worse. Much as I'd like to tell you there are secret moves you can master that will keep you safe from persecution all your life, the best you can hope for is to thrive in spite of whatever's thrown at you. In this chapter, we'll talk about prejudice, oppression, and violence, the physical and emotional toll they can take, and the resources available to help you stay safe and healthy, so you can keep on fighting the good fight.

Family Feud

They say change starts in the home, but unfortunately, so do bigotry, discrimination, and alienation. While straight people en masse are becoming more open-minded and respectful of LGBTQ identities than ever before, many LGBTQ folks can attest that the painful cliché of coming out only to be rejected by your family of origin is still all too real.

If, upon your disclosing your LGBTQ status (or being outed), your family cut you off or demanded that you suppress your true self in order to stay in the fold, let me stress that they are small-minded and cruel. There is nothing wrong with you. You're worthy and smart, and you deserve the unconditional love of a family who values every part of who you are. If the people who raised you aren't holding up their end of the bargain, that is tragic, but it is not your fault. No matter what else you do, continue to remind yourself over and over that your identity is valid, that you matter, that you are worthy of respect and affection, and that you will find it. Familial rejection hurts, no doubt about it, but it doesn't have to destroy you.

It can, however, put you in a pretty serious emergency situation, particularly if you live with them or depend on them financially. If you find yourself without a safe place to stay, call the Safe Horizon youth homelessness hotline at 800-708-6600. They should be able to direct you to an LGBTQ-friendly shelter and other resources you might need to regain your footing. The Ali Forney Center has also compiled a directory of resources that may be useful, although they don't cover every state in the US. You can search the list at aliforneycenter.org/get-help/resources-by-state. If you're trans, genderqueer, or nonbinary, try the Transgender Housing Network at transhousingnetwork.com, where you can post a request for temporary housing or browse the "have couch" ads people have shared.

Unfortunately, the supply of LGBTQ-friendly shelters doesn't always keep pace with the demand, especially if you're outside of a major metropolitan area. In that case, you'll need to depend on friends, extended family, and informal queer social networks (both online and in person) to help you find a place to stay until you get on your feet. Always remember that there is no shame in asking for help when you need it, and even people you don't know that well may show their support in unexpected ways. You might be surprised how happy most people are to lend a hand, or a foldout couch.

If you think your family won't react well to the truth about your identity, as we discussed in Chapter 1, there's no shame in waiting to come out to them until you've saved up some money and are prepared to move out and support yourself. You don't owe anyone information that could be used to isolate or hurt you. But it's not healthy to get stuck in a long-term holding pattern, repressing a vital facet of your life so that you can continue having access to your family's material and emotional support. A short-term compromise can be the right choice, but you should be working to establish other ways of taking care of yourself so you don't have to live in the closet forever. You're going to start getting cramped in there. Plus, there's not a lot of room for your girlfriend.

Overt rejection is not the only danger of coming out to an

intolerant family, of course. Like many queers, you may have family members who would never come right out and say "You can't date girls and live under this roof," but rather gradually wear away at your patience and self-esteem with sidelong comments and insinuations that your identity is less worthwhile than other ways of being. This manifests in all kinds of ways: the mother who keeps mentioning how sad it is that she'll never have grandchildren (as though the technology to help reproductively incompatible couples become parents doesn't exist), the aunt who refuses to use the words "lesbian" or "girlfriend" but insists on asking how your "roommate" is doing, the cousin who casually describes everything he doesn't like as "gay."

If everyone around you behaves this way, it's unsettlingly easy to let them convince you that their homophobic attitudes are not a big deal, or that you'll be the asshole if you make a big deal out of it. But if it's hurting you, it matters, even if you're the only one who thinks so. Don't feel that you have to let other people's microaggressions slide in the name of being the bigger person. There's nothing wrong with standing up for yourself and your needs, and anyone who tells you otherwise is either misguided or just a jerk.

How you stand up for yourself will vary based on your personal circumstances and relationship with your family, but whatever you do, remember that it's okay to have and enforce your boundaries, even if your family doesn't understand why you have them and even if enforcing them hurts someone's feelings. People might try to make you feel that you're being unreasonable because your needs conflict with what they want for you. Don't give in to their version of reality. You need what you need, and that's okay. Protecting your physical and emotional health comes first.

If you can talk to your family about how their behavior hurts you, and guide them toward more positive ways of speaking and interacting, that's great—whether it involves calmly and sweetly explaining why their past actions have been hurtful, or going red in the face and screaming "Stop using that word or I will *never speak to you again.*" If no amount of cajoling or ultimatums can persuade them to stop saying things you find offensive, perhaps you can compromise on simply avoiding the topic. But in some situations, compromise doesn't work, education doesn't take, and the daily toll of living with willful and oppressive ignorance becomes unbearable. In this scenario, you may have to take the initiative in decreasing contact with your family—or cutting them off entirely—until and unless they educate themselves.

I don't make that suggestion lightly. I know that even if the relationship is deeply fraught, separating yourself from your family of origin is difficult and painful and may not even feel possible. Remember, though, that no one is ever entitled to a relationship with another person—it has to be earned through respect, affection, dependability, and kindness. A family that refuses to treat you how you want and deserve to be treated is violating their contract with you. Walking away from them doesn't make you bad, ungrateful, or cruel. It makes you a strong person who is taking the necessary steps to protect yourself.

And if you do walk away from the people who raised you, you still won't be alone. There is a world full of LGBTQ and allied people out there, many of whom would be thrilled to share support, friendship, and mix CDs with you. While you're mourning what you've lost, don't forget to be excited for what's ahead.

Take Your Queerness to Work Day

While most of us have the ability—however painful it might be—to walk away from our families of origin, walking away from an unsafe or discriminatory workplace is not always even an option. You can live without a family for a lot longer than you can live without a job, unless you have a sugar mama or are independently wealthy (and if you are, would you consider making a philanthropic donation to the Queer Advice Columnists with Crushing Student Debt Foundation?). Even if your workplace isn't LGBTQ-friendly, cutting your losses and walking away is challenging, especially if the rent is due next week.

Just like it's okay to stay closeted to your family while you strive to become independent from them, it's fine to keep your orientation or gender a secret in the workplace while you try to find another job. Even in states where sexual orientation and gender identity are protected classes (meaning you can't be fired for being gay, bi, or trans), insensitivity and thoughtlessness from people who don't know how to deal with LGBTQ folks can cause a lot of discomfort and unhappiness and make it hard to get through the workday. If you're afraid that might happen to you, there's nothing wrong with keeping to yourself while you focus on finding a job in a more diverse and accepting workplace.

In states that don't offer legal protection for orientation

or gender identity, you may still be protected by the laws in your city or the policies of your company. It's always a good idea to look into the rules governing a particular area or organization before accepting a job there. If your company has an HR department, speaking with them should give you a clearer understanding of your options. Even if your state protects LGBTQ people from employment discrimination, those protections may not apply to some organizations, particularly if they're religiously affiliated. As frustrating and unfair as it is that the onus is still on LGBTQ people to protect ourselves from discrimination, doing plenty of research and knowing the regulations that affect your job is the best way to arm yourself against whatever gets thrown your way.

Be aware, too, that even in places where gender and orientation are not protected by law, you may have legal recourse if you are fired because of your LGBTQ identity. Contact the Lambda Legal Help Desk (lambdalegal.org/help/online-form) to find out more about your options in a specific legal situation.

If you don't think being open about your gender or orientation will endanger your job, but your workplace doesn't feel like a safe place to openly be yourself, it may be worth pursuing ways to improve the environment for yourself and other LGBTQ people. Can you talk to HR about articulating a clearer anti-harassment policy? Can you convince your boss to require more inclusivity and sensitivity training for employees? Are there other queer folks in the office with whom you can band together to chat about life and ways to make the workplace better for everyone? Anything you can do to improve things at your job won't just make your life run more smoothly; it will make other queer people safer and happier, even after you've moved on to bigger and better things.

Because a job is more or less a necessity for survival, many of us can't afford to be as choosy as we'd like regarding the organizations to which we devote our time and energy. Still, if your job doesn't have a welcoming climate or doesn't value you for the person you are, it's probably worth it to look for a different position. Changing societal attitudes about LGBTQ people are making their way into American workplace culture, and it's very likely that an opportunity exists that would be a better fit for you.

In the meantime, if you have to hide a part of your identity at work for the sake of comfort or job security, it's all the more important to build a strong support system for yourself outside of work. Make sure you have someplace you can be authentically yourself and unwind from the stress of keeping secrets from nine to five. Fulfilling hobbies, friendships, long walks with your dog—these are the things that will keep you sane, at least until we manage to bring the entire exploitative machinery of capitalism crumbling down around us.

School of Hard Knocks

Though coming out later in life is neither uncommon nor unacceptable, many—perhaps most—LGBTQ people figure out their identities in high school or college. (Lots of us know earlier, but we often don't have the words to describe what we feel until our teen or early adult years.) This means that our experiences with those institutions are crucial to shaping our sense of how we move through the world as queer people—

and, often, how we deal with a world that doesn't value us as we deserve.

Unfortunately, high school can be nightmarish for LGBTQ kids, who are much more likely than the average population to experience bullying. Think about how terrible we all know high school is, and then realize what it means that for queer and trans kids it's *even worse*. The good news (if you've got a fairly low bar for "good") is that the misery has an expiration date. After the teen years, bullies tend to move on from name-calling, backpack-stealing, and outright assault to more subtle forms of harassment, in part because they can now be tried as adults. Just like all those YouTube videos claim, it really does get better for almost everyone when they move on to college or a career, or just get the fuck out of Dodge.

If you are suffering through a high school experience that feels like being trapped in a zoo for sociopaths, and the adults in your life are insisting that it can't be that bad—or worse, that you're bringing mistreatment on yourself by refusing to be normal—I beg you to hold tight to these two facts: One, it is as bad as you think it is. Your feelings are valid, and if you're in pain, it's not an overreaction. There is nothing wrong with you for hating what's happening; there is something wrong with the system around you, a system that frequently penalizes victims for making waves rather than punishing the people who actually cause harm. And the second thing to remember is that it will end. If you feel ashamed, if you feel miserable, if you feel scared, those feelings are a product of your environment, not inextricably linked to who you are. They will not follow you forever. They will be with you until you graduate, but then you will outrun them and go on to things so bright and new you'll hardly believe it. Promise yourself that you will get to the other side, because the best way to say "fuck you" to everyone and everything that's hurt you is to survive in spite of them.

I'm not going to promise that one day the pain you've gone through won't matter anymore. It will always matter. It will always be part of you. Suffering changes you in ways that can't be undone. But one day you will look back and it will be behind you, and in the context of your whole beautiful life it won't be as big as it seems right now; it will just be one of many things you have survived. This means that, right now, the most important thing you can do is survive.

If you can stand it, you should finish school. According to GLSEN's 2013 National School Climate Survey, "given the hostile climate faced by LGBT youth in general, and transgender and gender nonconforming students especially, these students may . . . be at higher risk of being pushed out or dropping out of school." Being driven out of school by harassment and bullying is one of many ways queer and trans folks are set up to struggle in life, to lag behind our straight and cis counterparts and spend our lives catching up instead of kicking ass. I don't want that to happen to you. I want you to power through it, scrape off the bullshit, and rule the world. Your high school diploma is the key to a whole new life of possibilities, and you deserve to make the most of every single one of them.

But if the loneliness and the hurt are wearing you down inside, if they are making you less the person you know you should and can be, if you simply don't believe you can keep getting up and walking headlong into the misery five days a week, then it's okay to cut and run. There is something in you that wants to live, and knows what must be done to make that possible. Listen to your gut. Trust it. Go where it sends you. There will be time later to go back and get your GED, as long as you make it to the other side of today.

Whether you stick it out or run for the hills, you'll need to start looking for sources of support, building yourself a community you can lean on. Asking for help isn't a display of weakness; in fact, a willingness to be vulnerable in order to get what you need is a form of strength. If you can, start by talking to your family of origin. Having parents or siblings or a trusted aunt who knows what you're going through, who listens to your troubles and reassures you regularly that you are important and understood and loved, can go a long way toward lightening the psychological load of bullying and harassment. If you don't have someone in your family you can talk to, look for a trustworthy adult—a teacher, a school counselor, a therapist, a coach, etc. This person may or may not be able to intervene and advocate on your behalf with your school, but at the very least, they will be able to provide the perspective of someone who made it through their own tumultuous adolescence (everyone's adolescence is tumultuous; anyone who says differently is a robot in disguise). They should be able to sympathize with what you're going through, help you develop some coping mechanisms, and, most important, remind you of your potential value. If you're lucky enough to find a really good mentor, they may even be able to

help you identify and take the first steps toward your illustri-
ous future. Make sure to thank them in your bestselling auto-
biography.

And begin looking for allies among your peers, because
chances are good you're not the only LGBTQ student in your
area. If your school has a Gay-Straight Alliance or equivalent
organization, join it! You'll make friends, get involved in important political causes, learn more about queer culture, maybe
even score a date or two. If there's no such club at your school
yet, it might be worth the effort to start one. My friend Mikey
started a GSA our freshman year of high school, and by the
time we graduated we had not only hosted a citywide high
school GSA conference but had thrown some of the greatest
slumber parties this world has ever seen. Visit gsanetwork.org
for more information and resources on how to create a GSA
at your school. The work you do today could make all the
difference in another LGBTQ kid's life.

The Delicate Art of the Drive-By

Even if you're bizarrely fortunate and your family, school,
and workplace accept you as you are without question, I'm
sorry to say there's pretty much no chance you'll make it
through life as a queer person without anyone ever being a
dick to you. The only way to accomplish that is to be completely stealth, out to literally no one, and while it might be a
little safer, what a lonely and small life that would be. You
deserve to live fearlessly and vibrantly. Unfortunately, doing
so will sometimes make you a target for the small-minded
and frightened. Existing while visibly female is already dan-

gerous enough, as pretty much every woman or woman-adjacent person can attest. When you add queerness or gender nonconformity (or being a person of color, or a fat person, or . . . well, just about anything) to the mix, a certain breed of quasi-human will feel compelled to put you in your place, to remind you that it's still their world.

Let's be very clear about this: It's not. It's your world. It's our world. It belongs to everyone who is brave and honest and loving and weird and ready to be their authentic selves and create new ways to live. The people who hate you are afraid that you know that; they're afraid you'll stop being meek and start taking over the earth, and they want to intimidate you into submission before you can realize your potential.

Don't let them do it. I'm not saying "Ignore harassment and it will go away." It won't, and it does none of us any good to pretend. You need to acknowledge the discrimination you face in order to take the necessary steps to keep yourself and your community safe. But don't give in to the haters' version of the world, or of you. Protect yourself without living in fear.

Drive-by harassment takes many forms. It can be a literal drive-by—someone yelling a slur at you from a passing car, or, less frequent but more upsetting, throwing things. This sucks and is scary, but it's usually over quickly with no further engagement required. Feel free to flip them off or yell something back, especially if you're in a populated area—I usually do.

Pedestrian-on-pedestrian hassling can be scarier, especially when some creepy dude (it's almost always a dude) actually starts following you. There's not a perfect way of dealing with this. You can tell him to fuck off, but that might escalate the situation. You can pull out your phone and threaten to call the cops—or actually call them, if you feel comfortable doing so. You can call a friend and stay on the phone with them until you reach your destination or a safe (populated, well-lit) place. You can also anticipate that these situations will arise and make prior arrangements to defend yourself, whether that means traveling in a pack, taking martial arts classes, or attaching a canister of Mace to your key chain.

Taking precautions to protect yourself is great, but it's also crucial to keep in mind that sometimes bad people do bad things, and it's not your fault. It's not your fault if there was something you could have done to avoid it; it's not your fault if you could have fought back harder. Your job is to survive, and that includes not tearing yourself down for the misfortunes that befall you. Neither should you fall into the trap of thinking you have no right to be upset about the people who have hurt or harassed you because others have had it worse. Your feelings are real and they matter. Owning them, honoring them, and working through them is how you keep them from destroying you. And if your survival doesn't seem like enough of an endgame in itself (again, I want to remind you that it really, really is), remember that living well—and for a long, productive time—is the best revenge.

Our Own Worst Enemies

Of all the injustices and indignities perpetrated upon marginalized people by a heterosexist and cissexist (not to mention patriarchal and racist and classist) society, I think my least favorite might be the way it turns us into weapons against ourselves. The stress and trauma of living in a world that's set up to keep the outsiders—that would be us, babes—on the outside eventually penetrates even the thickest skin. It gets us thinking, *Maybe there really is something wrong with me. Maybe that's why they treat me this way.* Or if we don't concede our intrinsic worth, at the very least we start to think, *A life with this much suffering is not worth it.* So we begin—consciously or subconsciously—to sabotage ourselves.

LGBTQ people have higher-than-average rates of depression, suicide attempts, and dropping out of high school, and we have worse health outcomes across the board than our straight and cis counterparts. We also have disproportionately high rates of drug and alcohol abuse. *Well, no goddamn wonder,* you're probably thinking. It's rough out here. Who can blame us if we need a little chemical assistance to make it through—or if we just can't make it through at all? But there comes a time when your vices, whatever they are, no longer keep you going—instead, they hold you back. Whether you drink them, smoke them, or date them, you need to find a way to shake them off so you can move forward unencumbered. If you don't, if you hurt yourself or stay in a situation that you know is hurting you, you're just doing the Man's work for him. You're keeping yourself down.

That's not to say that addiction or mental or physical illness is something you can just decide you're done with, where you recite some inspirational mantras in the mirror every morning, do a little yoga, and move on. The power of positive thinking is not enough to overcome the very real stress, trauma, and oppression you're living with. You've probably had a lot of years of hardship in which to develop your arsenal of coping mechanisms. It's going to take plenty more work to dismantle those weapons—or to at least stop pointing them at yourself. But it's good work, important and necessary. Think of yourself as a job that you love and want to get ahead in, or, if climbing the career ladder isn't your jam, maybe a gorgeous classic car that you're restoring to perfect condition.

It can be hard to get into the habit of treating yourself well, taking good care of yourself physically and emotionally. The insidious trick of mental illness is to convince you that you're not sick at all—that you really deserve to be miserable and unwell, that happiness isn't within your universe of possibilities. It's not true. The inner voice that tells you this is a nasty little lying monster, and with practice you can stare it down and take its power away. (Does it sound like I know what I'm talking about? I don't, really. Every time I have an anxiety attack I am fully convinced that I am not actually having an anxiety attack—I'm just calmly assessing the facts and arriving at the rational and justified conclusion that *I am a total failure and nothing will ever be okay*. But I'm working on it!)

Imagine that instead of yourself, the person struggling with these issues is your best friend or your little sister. Tell yourself what you'd tell her: You're amazing, you matter, you deserve to feel better. Give yourself little treats as encouragement and as a reward for keeping up the good work: a walk in the sun, a delicious homemade meal, tickets to that trashy action movie you'd never admit you're dying to see. Cut yourself some slack. Getting better isn't easy, and it's fine if you skip folding the laundry on occasion while you're getting there.

And ask for help. You can probably find a therapist within your price range (there are lots who charge on a sliding scale), and if you're struggling with mental illness, substance abuse, or toxic relationships, it's very much worth pursuing professional assistance. A good therapist will work with you to set goals and keep track of your progress. If the first therapist you find isn't a good fit, it's fine to look for someone new and start over; not liking your doctor doesn't mean you're beyond help or that therapy is pointless.

If professional mental health care is not an option, at least make sure you've got a solid support system. Your allies can help you be a better ally to yourself—don't be afraid to reach out to them. No one gets up this mountain alone.

Behind Closed Doors

When the world tells you you're a second-class citizen, it makes sense to retreat into the comforting embrace of people who are like you, people who get it, people who don't see you as a walking, talking Gay Agenda but as a dynamic and unique human being. As queer folks, our relationships and communities with other queer people are what sustain us. They're our anchor. Which makes it all the more difficult to extricate ourselves when they cause us harm.

Physical, emotional, and sexual abuse can happen in queer relationships. We're used to intimate-partner abuse being portrayed as male-on-female, and while that is the most common dynamic, female and nonbinary abusers absolutely exist. Some queer folks are hesitant to define what their partner does as abuse, because they've never seen examples of partner violence between LGBTQ folks and don't recognize it when it happens to them. Know that it's a possibility, and be on the lookout for warning signs. If you feel afraid of your partner, if you're frequently unhappy in your relationship but can't speak up because of how she'll react, if she pressures you to do things you don't want to do (sexually or otherwise), and, of course, if she hurts you physically or is generally violent, there's a good chance your relationship is abusive and you should be figuring out how to get out of it. Remember, you're a bomb-ass person who deserves safety and happiness. You know in your heart of hearts when you're not safe and happy. Listen to that inner voice, and if it says to go, go.

Queer people and communities are tragically underserved when it comes to resources for domestic violence and abuse survivors. Some states in the US (including New York, Virginia, and Arizona) don't allow people to get a restraining order against a same-sex partner. In many places, trans women are barred from accessing women's shelters and other forms of support intended for female survivors. And even when you're not officially prohibited from getting the assistance you need, cultural insensitivity and incompetence from health care providers and social workers can make accessing it stressful, if not impossible. If you can avail yourself of legal recourse or state support in getting out and back on your feet, by all means do so. If not, draw on informal support systems—your family, friends, and broader community. You can also contact the National Coalition of Anti-Violence Programs (ncavp.org) to find out what resources are available to violence survivors in your area.

Unfortunately, because it so often feels like it's us against the world, some queer communities are reluctant to alienate one of their members by "taking sides" in cases of abuse. Condoning the actions of an abuser is far from universal, but it's still entirely too common. If, in trying to seek support to get out of an unsafe situation, you are met by suggestions to "hear the other side" or "work this out calmly," the people you're talking to are not your true friends—they are cowardly creatures who value nonconfrontation over justice. They're probably the same people who talk about how much they hate "drama," and by "drama" they mean "other people having the nerve to inconvenience me with their emotions." It's hard and painful to find out that your friends aren't there for you when you need them most, but you'll also find out in these moments whom you can truly depend on. Clarity is a gift in the long term, even when, in the short term, it really, really sucks.

It's also possible that some people—either your abuser or others within the LGBTQ community—will pressure you to stay silent about your experience, lest it make gay people look bad or otherwise hurt the Cause. Do not be misled; anyone who says this is twisting and polluting the Cause to suit their own nefarious ends. Liberation for queer people cannot come at the expense of the most vulnerable among us. The end-game for LGBTQ civil rights is not to convince the world that our community is one big homogenized mass of good-natured rainbow-flag-waving awesomeness. It's to be seen and judged on our merits—or flaws—as individuals. A movement that demands your silence is not a healthy movement, and it's not one that will survive much longer.

Who You Gonna Call?

I've talked a lot in this chapter about the importance of community, of informal support networks that stand in for the more official resources from which LGBTQ people are too often excluded. But how do you find that community? We discussed some strategies in Chapter 2, so I won't rehash them here, but I do want to talk about how to find not just people to socialize with but friends you can truly depend on.

Just because someone is queer doesn't automatically mean they'll have your back through thick and thin. Work to nurture friendships that go beyond just enjoying each other's company. This is a quality-over-quantity game—it's better to have one true-blue lesbro than a bunch of people you can get margaritas with but can't talk to about anything serious. The best way to develop friendships that will get you through the tough times is to be the kind of friend you're looking for. Be honest, be trustworthy, be willing to go an extra mile—or an extra hundred—to make sure the people you love are safe and happy. This doesn't mean you should allow yourself to be taken advantage of; it just means that if you're generous with your time and affection, some people—worthwhile people— will give back what they get from you.

Some people will repay your kindness with thoughtlessness or indifference, but it doesn't necessarily mean you need to cut them out of your life. A mediocre person can still be fun to hang out with. Just be aware of their weaknesses so you don't try to lean on them when you're truly hurting. A friend who consistently doesn't listen to you, bails on plans, or tells you that whatever's bothering you "isn't that big a deal" is someone who won't be there when the going gets tough. There's no surefire way to know which people you can count on to see you through the worst until it happens, but bet on the friend who always takes your side in small ways and goes out of her way to remind you that you're important and loved.

If your social circle is more about watching the football game together than providing unflagging emotional support, you can still find ways to reach out when you're struggling. If there's an LGBTQ community center near you, contact them to find out whether they have a sliding-scale therapy or group counseling program you could join. But even without physical access to groups and people that can support you, there's always the Internet. Geographically and socially isolated LGBTQ folks are finding it more and more possible to connect with people online to offer each other encouragement, advice, and real, tangible help. Look for blogs by people who have been through what you're going through, or start your own. Find community in the comments sections of websites you love, and ask those people for suggestions on where else to look. Don't make the mistake of thinking that an online community is less "real" or less valid than a physical one; you'd be denying yourself a huge source of friendship and even empowerment.

Online communities don't just provide a shoulder to cry on. I've seen Internet friends rally to find someone who was kicked out of their home a place to sleep, track down job-search resources for gender nonconforming folks, and raise money for medical care that wasn't covered by insurance. Don't assume that just because you've never met someone face-to-face, they don't have your back.

Reaching Out, Reaching In

The LGBTQ community's continuing ability to thrive, to support each other, to grow and evolve and find new ways of kicking ass generation after generation, is due in large part to the fact that people recognize the importance of giving back to the Cause. After you've made it through the hardest times, when things really do start getting easier (if it hasn't happened yet, I promise it will—just stick with us a while longer), it's your responsibility to reach back from your place of relative stability and safety and offer a hand to the people who are still trying to get there.

We owe it to each other to help each other survive. We also owe it to the world. This planet needs a healthy, well-adjusted crop of queer and trans folks and others who see life beyond the arbitrary restrictions of gender binaries and compulsory heterosexuality, because they're the ones who are going to create more honest and satisfying ways of being. We have to keep each other going long enough to get to that point.

Everyone has heard plenty of times that "it gets better," but that doesn't happen by accident. It's true that, these days, your life as an LGBTQ person is likely to improve as you get older, escape childhood bullying, and learn to advocate for yourself. That wasn't the case fifty years ago. The only reason it's possible to tell today's youth that things will get better is because the generations that came before us worked hard to *make* it better. They marched, they fought, they wrote, they helped each other through the thick of it, and they created a better world.

But not a perfect one. It's not yet time to abandon the fight. To do so would disrespect the pain and sacrifice that led us to this point. There is still plenty of work to be done, and if we don't do it, no one will.

When you're in a dark place and you're not sure you're going to make it, your job is to survive, whatever it takes. But once you've emerged and the light is shining again, your job is to keep others safe to the best of your abilities. That means helping to educate people on the truth of queer lives and the validity of queer experiences until familial rejection and school bullying are things of the past. It means protesting, donating, calling your representative, organizing, and otherwise fighting for LGBTQ people's rights to marriage, health care, employment, housing, and protection under the law. It means fighting to make the queer spaces you enjoy as inclusive and intersectional as possible, and taking an active stance against biphobia, transphobia, racism, classism, and misogyny in the LGBTQ community. It means seeking out and supporting artists and creators who are LGBTQ. It means offering emotional support to your friends and family members who are struggling, and, when possible, giving advice from your own experience.

Basically, it means not kicking back and congratulating yourself on how far you've come. I don't mean that you don't deserve congratulations for making it this far—I'm really proud of you, and so glad you're here with us. Take a breather if you need to. Have a cup of tea. Take a really cute selfie.

Then it's time to get back to work.

Chapter 9

❧

If You Liked It, Then You Should Have Put a Ring on It: Marriage

Marriage equality is easily the most talked-about LGBTQ rights issue of the early twenty-first century. While the political implications of same-sex marriage capture a great deal of attention, marriage is also a deeply personal decision, affecting both private and public life. And though it's often portrayed as an us-versus-them issue—in one corner, equality-loving queers clamoring for their right to walk down the aisle; in the other, bigots insisting on "one man and one woman"—the truth is that many LGBTQ people have decidedly complicated, ambivalent, or even negative feelings about marriage. In this chapter, we'll sort through some of these feelings and discuss how to decide when or whether you want to get married, the care and keeping of a relationship you hope will last the rest of your life, the many different definitions of the word "family," and why marriage isn't the finish line in our race toward liberation. Do you take A Queer Chick to be your lawfully nonbinding and nonexclusive source of life advice and sex jokes for as long as we both shall live? If you don't, you can still have some of this cake.

The Last Person You'll Ever See Naked: When to Get Married

So you've been together for a few months or even a few years, you did the U-Haul thing, and the sound of her snoring is so familiar and soothing you actually sleep better with it than without it. But how do you know whether you have a long-term future together? Are you ready to get married? Do you even want to?

While the basic reasons for tying the knot are usually similar from one couple to the next—*I love you, I want to be with you forever, I think you're going to age really well in a silver-fox kind of way*—the specific details are so personal and unique that you'd probably be hard pressed to explain them to anyone else, even your partner. Only you can decide when it's the right time to pop the question. But if you're thinking about spending the rest of your life with somebody, take some time to consider what your reasons are, and whether they're likely to lead to lasting happiness.

You should make a lifelong romantic commitment to another person (whether that commitment is marked by a public celebration or simply whispered under the covers late at night) only when you're certain that you love her, love being around her, have compatible goals, values, and dreams, and want to support each other in every way you can. You should get married because you're crazy about each other and will each joyfully make compromises and sacrifices for the sake of the other's happiness and well-being. You should get married because you smile so big your face hurts when you happen to see her favorite brand of ice cream in the grocery store. Anything else is simply not enough.

You shouldn't get married just because you've been together for a long time and everyone's asking when you'll finally get hitched, or because your parents expect you to walk down the aisle, or because you'll be more financially stable together than apart. When you're under that kind of external pressure, it can feel like a wedding is the easiest way out, but it's better to stand firm now so you don't have to go through the much more difficult process of extricating yourself from an unsatisfying marriage in the future. You also shouldn't get married because you want to have children, or to obtain a co-parent for your existing children. You can have and raise children on your own. While being a single parent is often hard and thankless, it's better to look to your friends and community for support than to have your children grow up with unhappily married parents.

And crucially, you shouldn't get married because you think it will solve a problem in your relationship. Marriage should be the declaration of the love you both already know exists, not the way to prove its presence. Couples who marry in the hopes of patching up a disagreement are invariably disappointed. Buying a white gown and making some promises will not rid you of your trust issues or her short temper. You'll be the same people you were before, with the same difficulties, only now the pressure to fix things will be greater because the cost of walking away is higher. Plus, let's not forget that planning a wedding is a notoriously stressful and exhausting process, requiring a great deal of compromise and communication with your partner. How are you going to agree on a florist when you can barely agree on what movie to watch? If you don't go into it with a solid foundation, planning a wedding can easily tear the two of you apart before you even make it to the altar.

If you're having doubts or misgivings about getting married, if you have to talk yourself into it, you're either not ready to be married at all, or this person is not right for you. But there's one exception: It's common to be afraid that your relationship will one day end, and to wonder whether it's worth getting married when you can't be sure it will last. That fear is normal, but you shouldn't let it dissuade you from saying "I do" if that's what you both want. Sometimes, even when you love each other and have the best of intentions, life intervenes and you end up separating. There's no definitive way to predict this, and no way to ensure it won't happen to you, but you don't have to be 100 percent positive that you'll be together forever in order to get married. You just have to be certain that you *want* to.

Permanent Cohabitation: Can't Live with 'Em, Can't Live Without 'Em

Learning to live with a romantic partner is a high-level Actual Grown-Up Skill that too often gets glossed over. I'm not talking about the first few months post-U-Haul, when you have occasional arguments over how often the sheets need to be washed or how late at night it's acceptable to watch television. In those heady early days, you might experience some relationship stress, but you're still mostly on your best behavior, putting on makeup regularly and holding in farts until the other person leaves the room. I'm talking about when you've been together for years, sharing your space and your time and getting to know each other at the deepest possible level.

It's hard to keep secrets from someone you're banging or someone you're living with, but when you're doing both with the same person, your privacy will dwindle until it's almost nonexistent. If you live with your partner, she will eventually know just about everything there is to know about you, including how much you whine when you're sick, which episode of *Veronica Mars* makes you cry, how long you're willing to pull clean clothes directly out of the laundry basket without putting anything away, and how bitchy you get when you're under pressure at work. She will, in short, become acquainted with the worst as well as the best of you. The mystery will disappear from your relationship.

But no mystery doesn't have to mean no romance. In fact, once the thrill of finding out new things about each other is gone, it's often replaced by a different kind of thrill—that of intimacy, of knowing each other better than anyone else ever has or will. Intimacy isn't always self-sustaining, however. If you want your relationship to survive this transition without being sidetracked by boredom and complacency, you'll need to put some time and effort into it.

When you see your partner all the time, it's extra important to express interest in and appreciation for each other. At the end of the day, don't just make a beeline for the kitchen; say hello, give her a hug and a kiss, and ask how her day was.

Let her know that you appreciate the things she contributes to your household, whether that's her paycheck, home-cooked meals, or a keen eye for eclectic yet cohesive decor. Spend time together doing dating-type things, not just watching the news and falling asleep; even if you're too broke for fancy meals or romantic vacations, you can go for bike rides or have a picnic dinner on your living room floor. Just because you're used to each other doesn't mean you should stop trying to sweep her off her feet, or at least sweep the kitchen.

Don't let the pilot light go out on your sex life, either. Remember that whirlwind of boning when you first started living together, having sex any time of the day or night, going through elaborate rituals of attraction just to get each other in bed? Now, though you might still have sex any time of the day or night, the seduction has probably been reduced to one of you saying "Hey, want to bone?" while flossing your teeth. Although it's normal to fall into a sexual routine when you've been together for a while, it's important not to make your partner feel like you take her for granted. Find little ways throughout the day to let her know that you still think she's wildly attractive and that you're excited to have her around.

Lesbian Bed Death: The Struggle Is Real(ish)

One of the big concerns of long-term lady couples is the dreaded Lesbian Bed Death, an awful term coined in the 1980s to describe the supposed tendency of queer women to stop having sex altogether after a few years of dating. I don't know very many girl-on-girl couples who haven't wondered, after a night or two without orgasms, whether the LBD (which sounds like some kind of lethal disease) was finally coming to claim them. So let's talk about exactly how real Lesbian Bed Death is, and how it can be avoided.

First of all, it's worth noting that almost all couples get it on less frequently after five years than they did when they first started dating. When you have a new girlfriend, everything is fresh and exciting and urgent, and you're tearing each other's clothes off every chance you get, but that kind of energy is unsustainable for most of us. As you continue on your path together, things like jobs and social commitments and the importance of getting at least six hours of sleep a night start to get in the way of your naked marathons, and you settle into a less demanding sex schedule. This is normal—it doesn't mean that you're falling out of love; it just means that you can't keep the honeymoon going forever.

Multiple studies have found that couples consisting of two women do tend to settle into a routine that includes less frequent sex than dude-lady or dude-dude couples—thus, the scientific basis for Lesbian Bed Death. However, more recent studies have found that while queer women might not get it on as often, our sex lasts longer and is more likely to be multiorgasmic than the sex other couples are having. Women in same-sex relationships also report about the same level of satisfaction with our sex lives as our dude-oriented counterparts. Generally speaking, then, we're all having sex that we enjoy—so why are we up in our heads about whether our sex lives are impressive enough to straight people?

The only thing you need to worry about is whether your sex with your partner is fulfilling for the two of you. If it's not, you can talk it out and decide what to do (is it a scheduling issue? Waning libido? Do you need to invest in a better strap-on harness?), but if you're fundamentally happy with how things are going crotchwise and you're just insecure about the possibility that some third party would think you're undersexed, you should probably let it go. I, too, occasionally get worried that somewhere in the world the Sex People are getting laid more than me, but then I remember that I love my partner and our relationship and our inventive and satisfying sex life. When you become more concerned about how your romance might sound to others than how it feels to the two of you, then and only then do the Sex People win.

The Process of Processing

If you haven't spent much time around queer women and queer women's culture, you might still think of the word "process" as a noun that means "a way of doing things." The more you hang out with (and date) lesbians, though, the more you'll start to think of it as a verb—one that means, approximately, "to talk about your feelings and another person's feelings and how those feelings interact with and affect each other, while using lots of 'I' statements and probably crying."

Processing sometimes gets a bad rap, but it's common in girl-on-girl circles for a reason, and not just because chicks love to share their emotions. Processing with someone you care about is relationship maintenance; it lets you check in on potential problems before they explode into fights, and it can help you identify the real issues festering beneath that one pointless argument you can't seem to stop having.

The difference between processing and what you might

simply call "talking things out" is that when you process, your goal isn't just to reach a compromise so you can stop being mad at each other. It's to identify the cause of the disagreement and drag it out into the open where you can look at it, poke it with sticks, and, ideally, realize that it's not so scary after all. It can feel like an agonizing waste of time when you'd rather just promise to take out the trash next time and leave it at that, and there are certainly people who overprocess (and demand overprocessing from their partners) because they enjoy the heightened intensity of it. Still, embracing processing can lead you to a deeper knowledge of your partner, a stronger understanding of yourself, and a more robust relationship overall.

If you're not one of the queer women (like me) to whom processing comes naturally, think of it as an interrogation of your own feelings. Say what you're thinking as clearly as possible, and avoid insults and words like "always" or "never." It's probably not true that your partner has never in her life done the dishes without being asked, and once you say that, she's going to feel defensive, and she'll be much less likely to hear what you have to say. Instead of going on the attack— "You left your dirty dishes in the sink again, you inconsiderate jackass"—try to explain what you're feeling and why: "When I notice that I'm doing way more of the housework than you, it makes me feel taken for granted."

When you process with your partner, keep in mind that this is not a fight and neither of you should be trying to "win." Instead, you should both have the same goal—to work through your issues and come to the best possible solution for your relationship. With that in mind, it's okay to take breaks, to walk away for a little while, and even to make each other laugh in the middle of a tough conversation. None of those things mean you've admitted defeat. You and your love are on the same team—it's the two of you against your own flaws, insecurities, and anything else that's holding you back from being the happiest, most functional goddamn couple this world has ever seen.

For people whose instinctive approach to conflict is to yell and storm out and sleep on the couch, processing will be scary. It's easier to lash out than to express the fear or sadness or vulnerability that's underneath your anger. But it's also much less productive. When you know where your fights are coming from, you have a much better chance of coming up with solutions that actually address the problem, rather than just slapping a Band-Aid over it and waiting for it to resurface in a new form. If you hope to grow together and use your disagreements as opportunities to strengthen your bond, processing is the best game in town.

Beginning practitioners are cautioned not to attempt to process at bedtime, lest you find yourself still awake and talking about your abandonment issues at four a.m. next Wednesday. Ignore conventional wisdom and go to bed angry. Your circadian rhythm will thank you.

Why Marriage Matters

Marriage is a deeply personal decision made between two people who want to share their hearts and joys and sorrows—that's obvious. But you can make that promise to each other at any time: after an evening of dancing, in bed late at night, on the couch while playing video games. No law or bureau-crat can take away the commitment you share with your tru-est, dearest smoochy-pants. So why is official recognition for same-sex marriage so important?

One reason, of course, is that marriage bestows so many tangible legal and financial benefits on couples, from sharing health insurance and inheriting property to being able to adopt each other's children easily and visit each other in the hospital. According to the Human Rights Campaign, there are 1,138 benefits, rights, and protections automatically granted to married couples. If two people who cannot legally marry wanted to set themselves up with equivalent protec-tions, they'd need a good lawyer, a lot of money, and a few years to fight the system to even come close.

But wanting to enjoy all the benefits of being legally rec-ognized spouses is not the only reason LGBTQ people have fought for marriage equality. Getting married is more than just a promise to your partner that you'll think her butt is cute even when she's eighty. It's a social contract. We cele-brate weddings with all of our friends and family because we want the people we care about to be as invested in our rela-tionship as we are.

When you invite someone to your wedding, you're not just hoping they'll get you that KitchenAid ravioli-maker at-tachment you've had your eye on. You're asking them to be a witness as you make one of the most important promises of your life and, in witnessing, to agree to hold you and your partner accountable for that promise. You're asking them to be your community in a real and active sense, to support you when times are hard, and to encourage you to work through it and keep your love alive. If we didn't need the support and recognition of our communities, there wouldn't be weddings at all—we'd just say our vows in the car on the way to brunch and save thousands of dollars. This is why even the smallest, most low-key city hall ceremonies have witnesses. Making a promise publicly gives it weight; it means that it matters not just to you but to your friends and loved ones. It means the people you care about see your love and your family as something worthy of celebration.

When same-sex couples are denied the right to marry, they're also denied that feeling of shared festivity, of communal acknowledgment that their relationship matters. Excluding queer people from marriage sends the message "You can do this, but you'll have to do it alone." That us-against-the-world mentality might seem exciting and romantic when you're in high school, but in the long term, it's just exhausting. The joys and burdens of romantic partnership are more joyful and less burdensome when they're shared, which is why prohibiting same-sex couples from getting married doesn't just rob them of important legal protections; it isolates them emotionally.

Just like anyone else, queer people want to know that we've got the support and encouragement of our family and friends during the defining moments of our lives. That's why marriage—not just as a private promise or a legal contract, but as a socially sanctioned milestone and occasion to party—is important. Well, that and the cake.

We Fought the Law

It's strange to think about how much the legal landscape surrounding same-sex marriage has changed in the last few years. Just a decade ago, when I was in high school, I thought marriage equality would happen within my lifetime, but probably not until I was middle-aged. Now, I'm twenty-seven (which, okay, I would have thought of as middle-aged when I was in high school), and same-sex marriage is legal in the United States. LGBTQ kids being born now will grow up in a world where they never have to question whether they'll be allowed to legally commit themselves to the person they love, and that's a beautiful thing.

My partner and I joke that we have five wedding anniversaries. There's the day we celebrated our wedding, with the traditional Big Fancy Party and white dress and elaborate dessert buffet and painstakingly curated reception playlist. We observe that as our official wedding anniversary each year, but it was totally symbolic, since our home state of Colorado didn't recognize same-sex marriage at the time. Our next anniversary is a little more than a week later, the date when, on our honeymoon in Massachusetts, we were legally married by a justice of the peace in a little park outside a suburban courthouse. But we could also count the day close to a year later when Colorado recognized same-sex civil unions, or the day when the federal government began recognizing all legally married same-sex couples regardless of their state of residence, or the day when Colorado, less than ten years after passing a constitutional amendment banning same-sex marriage, struck down that amendment and began issuing marriage licenses to queer couples. On every one of those dates, we laughed and cried and celebrated being one step closer to legitimate, one step closer to being just like everyone else. It took us a little more than two years to get from walking down the aisle to being officially married in every sense.

These days, you hear a lot of rhetoric about how marriage equality was always inevitable, that it was destined to happen at or around this point in time. There's talk about its opponents being "on the wrong side of history," as though today's events are already behind us. I think this is an error, as it erases the contributions of the generations of LGBTQ activists who fought and marched and protested and wrote letters and organized and gave their money and time to make this particular dream come true. For queer people growing up a generation ago, this seemed like an impossibly distant goal. Around the time I was born, LGBTQ activists were getting arrested for applying for marriage licenses in Colorado. By taking the reality of nationwide marriage equality for granted, we dishonor the struggle of all the people who came before us.

At Charlie's and my engagement party, my gay aunt (who used to pull me aside at Christmas to ask me very seriously whether I was doing okay, for reasons that did not become clear to me until later) approached me with tears in her eyes and said, "I never thought I would see something like this happening in my own family." This, more than anything, drove home how much the world has changed from one generation to the next. When she was growing up, she was never taught to see marriage as an option for someone like her. She lived with the same woman for decades, but they never got to create a bridal registry or have an official first dance together. Later, at my wedding, I crossed paths with my younger cousin, who had just come out as queer. "I'm so glad to see our whole family supporting you, because I know that means they'll support me, too," my cousin said. This is the historical moment that millennial queers occupy, poised between the triumph of the past and the hope of the future. The best thing we can do to honor this moment is appreciate how far we've come, and devote ourselves to the work that still needs doing.

More Than a Feeling: It's Not Just Marriage

Marriage dominates the current national conversation around LGBTQ rights to such an extent that you could be forgiven for thinking that marriage was the only item left to check off on the Gay Agenda before we subjugate the world to our diabolical queer will. However, the truth is that marriage equality is only a minor component of what must be achieved before queer and trans activists can call it a day.

Although the ability to marry one's chosen partner, regardless of gender, is an important step toward legal and social equality, it's hardly the only one left. LGBTQ students are still getting bullied and are still dropping out of school at astonishing rates, and a disproportionately high number of homeless teens are queer and/or trans. Queer and trans people are routinely barred from accessing resources they need to deal with homelessness, poverty, and physical and sexual abuse. Employment discrimination and housing discrimination still exist everywhere, even in places where they're technically illegal. Oppression and lack of support contribute to high rates of alcoholism, drug abuse, depression, and other mental illness. LGBTQ senior citizens are less likely to have social and familial networks to help them, and are more likely to live in poverty and have negative health outcomes than their straight and cis counterparts. LGBTQ people are still vulnerable to abuse and violence from many sides, especially trans women and extra-especially trans women of color, and many of us can't count on law enforcement to protect us, because law enforcement often overlooks or even participates in abuse against queer and trans people. Many of us struggle to find, much less afford, the health care we need, including HIV-related care, transition-related care, reproductive care, and mental health care.

I'm not bringing all of this up to discourage you or to dissuade you from fighting for marriage. But it's important that we as a community and movement don't lose our sense of perspective on what marriage equality really is: an important detail within a much broader picture. While legalizing same-sex marriage has provided tangible improvements in quality of life for many queer couples and their families, it's not the finish line by any stretch of the imagination. We won't achieve true equality until every member of our community is safe from persecution.

The prioritization of marriage has caused schisms in some queer communities, pitting folks who want to focus on marriage against folks who think other issues should come first. It's understandable that this would be a source of some conflict. Making a difference requires time and money and energy and person-power, resources that are always pain-fully scarce. If there's one particular cause that's nearest to your heart, it hurts to watch people devote themselves to other concerns when yours needs them so badly. But the truth is, we can't afford to put *any* of these crucial causes on hold while we focus all our strength on accomplishing one thing—not just because we'd never be able to agree on what that one thing should be, but because all of these questions are pressing and interrelated. What we as a community and as a society need is a whole bunch of passionate, compli-cated, engaged LGBTQ people working to make the world a better place.

Even if someone is working hard on a different cause than you are, that doesn't necessarily mean that they don't care about your cause. People are capable of caring about, and even working on, a lot of different things at once—in fact, scientists have not yet discovered an upper limit to the num-ber of things people can care about. Besides, someone who will be energetic and active in pursuit of one goal will proba-bly contribute to others as well.

You should absolutely do all you can to increase aware-ness of the issue that's most important to you, and get people involved. But don't attack people if they can't participate be-cause they're already committed elsewhere. The overall goal—a better, more just world for all of us—can only be achieved by lots of people pouring their hearts and souls into lots of differ-ent projects. Don't look at activism as a competition; instead, find ways to create connections and share resources with other invested, aware individuals. This work will not be fin-

ished in any of our lifetimes, but all of us have the ability—
and the responsibility—to do what we can.

Tolstoy Was Full of It

Even if you're a literary dilettante like me, you probably
recognize the line "Happy families are all alike; every unhappy family is unhappy in its own way," from *Anna Karen-
ina*. Far be it from me to criticize a brilliant and timeless work
of literature that I've never read, but on this particular point,
Tolstoy got it wrong as hell.

Though most of us who grew up in the Western world
were sold the same idyllic picture of familial bliss (heterosexual, monogamously married parents raising 2.5 of their bio-
logical children in a single-family home with a white picket
fence and a puppy), the truth is that that model isn't a source
of happiness for everyone. For some it's not an option at all,
while for others it might feel too restrictive. Some people
might initially want it but change their minds, depending on
the specific person or people they want to share their lives
with. In truth, there are infinite potential models for a happy
family, depending on the individuals involved.

There's a long tradition in queer culture and other marginalized communities of creating "chosen family," especially
for people who are alienated from their families of origin. A
chosen family is a group of people to whom you might not be
biologically or romantically connected, but with whom you've
decided to share your life, offering each other support and
love in a way that's closer and more interdependent than
mere friendship.

The meaning of "family" is so nebulous and ever-evolving that it's almost impossible to come up with a definition that will work for every permutation of the idea; the best I can do is to say that your family consists of the people who are most important to you, and to whom you are most important. Beyond that, it's up to you to determine who you want your family to be.

Your family can come together organically and without any planning, where you form bonds and then define them later, or it can be something you put thought and effort into creating. It's worth taking some time to think about what your ideal family would look like. Will your family be centered around a romantic relationship? If so, will you and your partner be monogamous? How will other romantic and sexual partners factor into your family-building efforts? Do you want to get married? Will you and your family live together? Do you want to raise children? Is it important that your children be biologically related to you, or are you interested in adopting? If your partner has children with another parent, will you participate in raising them? Do you envision being the breadwinner in your family, being a homemaker, or sharing those duties equally? Will your family of origin play a role in the family you build as an independent adult?

Bear in mind that the answers to these questions may change as you grow and learn things about yourself and what you need from the world. You may also want or need to reassess your priorities if you end up with a partner whose dreams of a family don't quite match yours. But being able to articulate what you hope for and why will give you a great foundation for discussion and negotiation as you begin building your family.

Your happy family might be a married lesbian couple with three kids from three different sperm donors, or a polyamorous triad with two children from previous relationships and a fourth partner who lives out of state, or a trans man deciding to get pregnant and become a single parent, or you and your best friend living alone next door to each other, or three generations of women in the same house—the possibilities are literally endless. Don't allow societal expectations to stand between you and the happiness you can share with the people you love. No two happy families are exactly the same, but that doesn't mean any of them are happier than the others. Be as creative as you want to be. As long as your family is built on bonds of love, respect, and support, it can look like just about anything.

Always a Bridesmaid

While marriage can be a source of great joy and stability and comfort and happiness, it certainly isn't always so grand. It's popular to encourage people, especially women, to pursue marriage as their ultimate goal (just yesterday I saw yet another "Why You Should Stop Looking for Mr. Right and Marry Mr. Okay" article making the Facebook rounds), but the fact is, not everyone wants to get married, and not everyone should. Whether you think you might like to get married someday but you haven't met the right person yet, or you feel that a legal contract has no place in your love life, or you're just not interested in spending the next however many years with one romantic partner, your choices are valid and important and deserving of respect.

One of the downsides of the recent momentum toward nationwide marriage equality is that in our haste to affirm the rights of people who want to marry, we risk reifying the idea that marriage is crucial for everyone. Suddenly, queer people who thought they'd escaped the pressure to wed are fielding questions like "So, when are *you* going to get married?" left and right. The wedding-industrial complex couldn't be more excited to reap the profits from same-sex weddings, and many of us who protested, campaigned, and donated so that queer people could have the *option* to marry are now realizing that what we've actually won might be the social assumption that marriage is mandatory and anyone who doesn't achieve it is failing—just like the cultural expectations unmarried straight people deal with.

If you're a marriage rights activist, it's important to make sure your rhetoric isn't marginalizing the lives and choices of the many queer people (and straight people) who aren't interested in marriage. Don't portray unmarried people as incomplete or tragic, and don't claim that people who don't marry can't have "real" families. Marriage is an option that should be available to anyone who wants it, but it's not mandatory, and the implication that you can't live a full and satisfying life without it is detrimental to many people in the LGBTQ community. It's important that we strike a balance between affirming the vital importance of marriage to some of us and acknowledging that it's not the endgame for everyone.

Fighting for your right *not* to marry is just as necessary as standing up for marriage equality for those who want to. Just as there's no true equality until everyone is safe from homophobic, transphobic, racist, misogynistic, and classist oppression and violence, there's no true liberation until we're all free to pursue the relationship and family models that bring us fulfillment and joy. If that doesn't include marriage for you, don't be ashamed of your decisions, and don't listen to anyone who tells you you'll "grow out of it." Yes, it's always possible that you'll change your mind or want something different later in life, but that doesn't mean your earlier choices were immature or wrong. (How often do we describe someone getting a divorce as having "grown out of marriage," after all?)

When people make assumptions about your relationship goals, it's okay to kindly but firmly say, "Jessica and I are really happy together, but I don't have any interest in getting married," or "No, I'm not looking for a girlfriend right now," or "As a matter of fact, I'm not planning to have kids." Don't feel like you have to apologize or make excuses for the things you want. Remember that whatever your reasons are, they're good enough—you don't need to get approval from anyone else to pursue your dreams.

As queer and trans people, we're used to our identities, relationships, and lives being the subject of excessive and unwarranted scrutiny, but that doesn't mean you owe anyone an explanation. You can choose to have a heartfelt talk about why your nontraditional relationship choices are healthy and right for you, or you can simply set a clear boundary—"I'm not interested in discussing this any further"—and walk away if it's not respected. Just make sure that you offer the people around you the same courtesy: Assume everyone has valid reasons for their choices, and don't treat other people's choices as less valuable just because they're not the ones you would make. Our differences are what make the world interesting. Plus, the more your friends get married, the more chances you have to catch a bouquet—you don't have to be interested in the symbolism of the tradition to enjoy free flowers!

Be Your Own Bridezilla

If, having considered all your options, you decide that getting married is the right choice for you, the next step will be planning your wedding. I am not remotely qualified to help you with that. Putting together a wedding can be an enormously complicated, stressful, and draining process, although of course it can also be as simple as checking online to see what time the county courthouse will be open tomorrow. There are entire books and websites dedicated to planning and pulling off your dream wedding, and if we got into the details, we'd be here all month. All I'll say is that you should prioritize, remember why you're getting married (to celebrate the love you and your partner share, not to show off your skill at arranging flowers in mason jars), and refrain from playing "The Chicken Dance" at your reception.

Weddings can be as traditional or as creative as you want them to be, but one thing is nearly universal: Just about every woman or woman-adjacent individual planning a wedding has experienced a moment when they thought, *Shit, am I being a bridezilla?* While the bridezilla stereotype, like all stereotypes pertaining to women, is largely based on misogyny and the invalidation of women's feelings, there can be a grain of truth to it. The media obsession with fairy-tale weddings leads to an enormous amount of pressure to make sure every detail is Pinterest-perfect, because *this is the most important day of your life!* And before you know it, you're having a screaming match with your intended over whether the napkins should be folded like fans or like swans, because your wedding photos are the most treasured keepsake you'll ever have and if the napkins aren't swans you might as well just throw the whole album in the garbage and set it on fire.

Obviously, that's excessive, and if you frequently find yourself in that kind of situation, you need to hire a planner or take yourself on a spa weekend or go for a long walk or do whatever else helps you calm down and reset your priorities. But there's something positive underneath the crazy, and tapping into it might just help you survive until your honeymoon.

Your wedding will probably not turn out to be the happiest day of your life. In fact, if you have a great relationship, your love and appreciation for each other will grow over the years until you're a hundred times happier than you were on your wedding day. Still, your wedding should—if you want it to—be one of the best parties you ever attend, and in order for it to live up to your (realistic) dreams, you're going to need the confidence to be your own advocate.

Even though this wedding belongs to no one but you and your partner, a lot of people are going to feel that they should have a stake in how it goes. Sometimes you'll have to take their needs and desires into consideration—don't force your butch BFF to wear a cocktail dress just because she's your person of honor—but more often, what you want and feel comfortable with takes precedence. It's not your job to live out someone else's dream of your wedding. This is especially true if some of the things you want to do are unorthodox or don't fit into the expected gender-binary pageantry. Don't want to be given away because it reinforces patriarchal assumptions about women as property? Skipping the invite to your homophobic great-aunt who hasn't spoken to you since you came out? Feel like getting married in matching white Doc Marten eight-eyes? These are totally legitimate and great choices even if they make some of your friends and loved ones uncomfortable, and you need to do what will make you feel happy and totally yourself on your special day.

Make sure to pick your battles, but be honest with yourself and the people around you, and don't allow anyone to overrule you on what's really important. Your sister got her nails painted navy when you specifically told her midnight blue? You can let that one slide. Your mom's threatening to boycott your ceremony if you go through with your plan to walk down the aisle in pants? That's when you need to stand up for yourself, set boundaries, and make it clear that you won't be steamrollered. It's your wedding, and as long as you're not asking people to violate their own boundaries or driving yourself mad making two hundred fifty calligraphy place cards by hand, what you say goes.

Keep Love Alive

No matter what choices you make about marriage, long-term relationships, and family, make sure you're always acting from a place of love. Get married because you love your partner, stay single because you love your independence, give your time and money to political causes because you love your community. Remember that what you love and what other people love may not always be the same, and be kind and understanding when someone does something you wouldn't have done. Sometimes love will lead you or others to make bad choices, or choices that have unforeseen consequences, but that doesn't mean the love itself is wrong.

Marriage equality is a major political issue throughout the United States and the world right now, but like many hot-button topics, it's ultimately a question of individuals wanting as many options as possible in order to make the best choices they can. You should neither get married nor skip getting married in order to make a political statement; you should do only what you truly feel is best for you and the people you care about. If you want to make the world a better place, I can think of few more effective ways to do that as a queer person than to pursue your own unique, personal, weird version of happiness as hard as you can. By going after your bliss without fear or apology, you'll be affirming and validating others' ability to do the same. Plus, people who are satisfied with their personal lives have approximately 76 percent more emotional energy, which they can then devote to sticking it to the Man.

Whatever you want, whatever you need, you have everything it takes to achieve it. I'm excited for you. I believe your life is going to be so thrilling and beautiful. I really do.

Chapter 10

∞

It's Not Good Enough Until
It's Amazing

You've made it to the end of this book, which means you are now a fully equipped, highly trained Queer Chick and can step forward into your enlightened, self-actualized life. From here on out, you're not going to have any problems....

Oh, wait, no, that's totally not true. This isn't a class you ever get to graduate from. You'll keep encountering new twists on old questions, over and over, throughout your life. You'll keep learning, and you'll pass on what you know, but you'll never quite be an expert. No matter how much you know, how much you've seen and experienced, how many times you've sworn not to make the same mistakes you've watched other people make, something will come along and totally knock you on your ass. Whether it's a new love, a new cause, or a new realization about yourself and your identity, when it hits, you'll have to start over from square one. You'll retrace the journey you thought you'd already taken, relearn the lessons you never thought you could forget.

And you know what? That's great. Sure, it's hard to make mistakes, to struggle and find your footing over and over again, to feel like you're the only one who doesn't know what's going on. But it's totally normal. Everyone is always learning new lessons and facing new challenges. If you reach a point in your life where you're no longer failing at anything, it means you're no longer pushing yourself.

As a queer person, you may sometimes feel like there are no road maps for your life, no role models you can follow to help you become the person you want to be. That can be lonely, and scary, but it's also freeing. You don't have to live up to anyone's expectations except your own. You can create the map you want, and let it lead you someplace unexpected, exhilarating, and quite possibly full of hot girls.

There's a lot of rhetoric in the mainstream LGBTQ rights movement about queer and trans people being "just like everyone else." I don't fully buy that. We're not worse or less natural or less deserving, but we are *different*. We experience the world slightly out of sync with the mainstream. Our desires, our needs, our loves, our identities set us apart. And that's a wonderful thing. It leads us to question whether "just like everyone else" is really what we want, to see beyond the social mores and expectations and go after our own particular idiosyncratic brand of bliss. At the very least, it gives us a chance to try.

What I want, more than anything, is for you to keep trying. I don't ever want you to become complacent, to settle for whatever you tell yourself is good enough. "Good enough" is something we all say too often, especially as marginalized people who have to fight until we're bloody for every tiny gain.

The fighting gets exhausting, and sometimes you ask yourself whether it's really worth it. Sometimes you think, *I deserve a break*. Sometimes you might be able to convince yourself that whatever you already have is good enough, if it means you can finally relax or stop pushing so hard.

It's a reasonable way to feel. You can't spend every day of your life fighting. You need and deserve to take time for yourself, to surround yourself with a loving support system of friends and family that make you feel good about who you are, to prioritize self-care. Spending time and energy on renewing yourself mentally and physically isn't just okay—it's the right thing to do. You can't contribute to the Cause when your soul is undernourished, or when you're stressed out to the point of total emotional breakdown. If you're thinking "I need a break," go ahead and take it.

But a break is all it should be. You should always have a dream toward which you're actively working—and once you achieve it, you should take a little time to celebrate your victory and then start working on something else. Looking around, propping up your feet, opening a beer and saying "Yep, this is fine" might be a great way to spend a weekend, but you'll get awfully bored—and boring—if you plan to spend the rest of your life that way.

The world, and even some of the people you love most, might try to tell you that what you have is good enough; that people like you can't live out those huge, awe-inspiring dreams, so it's better to just be satisfied with something small. I'm here to tell you that's a lie. You deserve the things you want the most, and you also deserve the passion and pride that come from working toward them until your body aches and your soul is singing. Whether your dream is to get married and raise children, or to end LGBTQ youth homelessness, or to be the best goddamn insurance inspector in your county—or all of those things, or something altogether different—you need to go after it and refuse to be satisfied with less.

I'm not saying you have to have the standard Big Dreams that Hollywood says will make you happy. You don't have to be striving toward all-consuming love or a glamorous career. Your goals can be little and strange and entirely your own. But once you've decided what "amazing" means to you— maybe not forever, but at this moment in your life—it's your job to go after it, not to ask yourself whether you should per-haps opt for something not quite as good but way more con-venient.

"Good enough" is a crusher of souls and a killer of dreams. People who commit to "good enough" relationships wake up years later lonely and angry and regretful and terri-fied that it's too late to find the real thing. (Great news: It's not!) People who spend their days at "good enough" jobs come home beaten down and hopeless. Telling yourself some-thing is "good enough" when it isn't what you really want is like telling yourself that one dry leaf of lettuce is a satisfying meal.

I'm not saying you shouldn't be realistic; we're not all go-ing to be rock stars or marry Ellen Page. Most of us will al-ways have day jobs and budgets and responsibilities and dirty dishes in the sink, but that doesn't mean our lives are mean-ingless. I'm saying you should never give up on searching for something so spectacular that it brings glitter and joy into every otherwise dull facet of your life. If you haven't found it or can't even imagine yet what it might be, that's okay. It's out there. It's going to rock your world.

Just don't fill all the space your dreams should occupy with things that are simply "good enough." Whatever it is, it's not good enough just because it's better than what you've had before. It's not good enough just because it's better than what your friends have. It's not good enough just because it's better than what previous generations got. It's not good enough just because it's a step in the right direction. Your life, in short, is not being graded on a curve. It's not good enough until it's amazing.

Acknowledgments

Thank you to Edith Zimmerman, who accepted a pitch from an unknown, unpublished baby writer and launched the column Ask A Queer Chick. Thank you to all the Hairpin editors who followed in Edith's footsteps—Emma Carmichael, Jia Tolentino, Haley Mlotek, and Jazmine Hughes—for giving Ask A Queer Chick an opportunity to develop, and thank you to the Hairpin readers and commenters who made it so much fun.

Thank you to everyone who's ever written to me with a question. I'm honored that you gave me those windows into your lives and hearts and allowed me to share my thoughts with you.

Thank you from the bottom of my heart to Jolie Kerr, both for inspiring me to make the leap from advice column to book and for introducing me to my agent. Thank you as well to the aforementioned agent, Kate McKean, to whom I owe eternal gratitude for her patience, guidance, and support.

Thank you to my editor, Kate Napolitano, for believing in *Ask a Queer Chick*, improving my manuscript a thousandfold, and making me cut down on my use of the word "awesome" by about 75 percent.

I would not be a writer if it weren't for Jana Clark: Thank you. I might be a writer without the Tucson slam family, especially Teresa Driver and Maya Asher, but I probably wouldn't be a very good one. Thank you. And thank you to Bhanu Kapil for turning me into a much weirder and more risk-taking writer than I ever would have been on my own.

Thank you to my beloved friends who cheered me on when I was overwhelmed, made me laugh when I was crying, and generally made me believe I could do this: Kate Lauer, Mandi Paley, Heather Goodrich, Dane Kuttler, Doc Luben, and Mickey Randleman. Thanks above all to Heather Mahoney Dacek, my other half. I hope if you could read this, it would make you proud.

Thank you to my family: my mother, Michelle Miller; my father, Ranger Miller; my siblings, Kara, Kevin, and Sam Miller; my stepmom, Dot Wright; and my mother-out-law, Patt King—your love and support mean the world to me.

And of course, always, my deepest and most profound thanks to Charlie King-Miller, who brings joy to every day of my life, encourages and supports me in going after my dreams, and makes the best lemon cheesecake in the entire world. I'm so lucky to have you cheering me on. I love you.

Resources

Whatever you're going through, you're not alone, and there are people out there who want to help! Whether you just want to know more about LGBTQ issues and people or you're trying to find your way through a crisis, the resources below will help you figure out your next move.

ONLINE

Advocate.com (The Advocate): LGBTQ news and enter-tainment

AfterEllen.com (AfterEllen): pop culture and news for gay, bisexual, and queer women

Autostraddle.com (Autostraddle): pop culture, news, and fun stuff for queer and trans women

Biresource.net (Bisexual Resource Center): support and awareness for the bi community

Blackgirldangerous.org (Black Girl Dangerous): writing by and for queer and trans people of color

Community.pflag.org (PFLAG National): support, education, and advocacy for LGBTQ people and their families and allies

Elixher.com (ELIXHER): news, politics, and writing by and for Black queer and trans women

Glaad.org (GLAAD): works to shape the narrative about LGBTQ people and provoke conversation that leads to cultural change

Gsanetwork.org (GSA Network): empowers and trains queer, trans, and allied youth leaders to advocate, organize, and mobilize an intersectional movement for safer schools and healthier communities

Lambdalegal.org (Lambda Legal): the oldest and largest national legal organization dedicated to achieving full recognition of the civil rights of LGBTQ and HIV-positive people

Lesbrary.com (The Lesbrary): reviews, recommendations, and links to books by and about queer women

Projectinform.org (Project Inform): information, inspiration, and advocacy for people living with HIV, AIDS, and Hepatitis C

Thetrevorproject.org (The Trevor Project): crisis intervention and suicide prevention for LGBTQ youth

Transhousingnetwork.com (Transgender Housing Network): connects trans people with safe temporary housing

BY PHONE

GLBT National Hotline (1-888-843-4564): peer counseling, information, and local resources

GLBT Youth TalkLine (1-800-246-7743): youth-specific (under twenty-five) peer counseling, information, and local resources

Lambda Legal Help Desk (1-866-542-8336): information and resources regarding discrimination related to sexual orientation, gender identity and expression, and HIV status

National Runaway Safeline (1-800-RUNAWAY, or 1-800-786-2929): support and information for those who are thinking of running away from home, those with friends who have run away, or runaways ready to come home

Project Inform HIV Health InfoLine (1-800-822-7422): support for questions and concerns about living with HIV

Trans Lifeline (1-877-565-8860): support for trans people in crisis

The Trevor Project (1-866-488-7386): crisis intervention and suicide prevention for LGBTQ youth

And of course, if you need advice (and don't mind waiting a few weeks to get it), you can always email me: askaqueerchick@gmail.com.